Journals

ALSO BY R.F. LANGLEY

Hem (infernal methods, 1978)
Sidelong (infernal methods, 1981)
Twelve Poems (infernal methods, 1994)
Jack (Equipage, 1998)
Collected Poems (Carcanet Press, and infernal methods, 2000)
More or Less (The Many Press, 2002)
Twine (Landfill, 2004)

R. F. Langley

Journals

Shearsman Books

Published in the United Kingdom in 2006 by
Shearsman Books Ltd
58 Velwell Road
EXETER
EX4 4LD

ISBN 978-1-905700-00-4

ACKNOWLEDGEMENTS

Some parts of this work have previously appeared in *P N Review*.

CONTENTS

Preface

These extracts are from a series of journals that I have been keeping since the 1970s. During the years they cover my parents have died, I have been divorced and remarried, our two children have been born and have grown up, found jobs, left home. None of this is mentioned in these pieces. This is not because I have chosen the extracts so as to avoid them, but because the journals are not the sort of journals that directly confront such things.

I was born in 1938, educated in Walsall and at Jesus College, Cambridge, and employed as a teacher, first at a grammar school at Shire Oak, in Walsall Wood, then at Wolverhampton Grammar School. The journals begin at this point. However I very seldom wrote about school life. There is only the occasional piece here which dips into it. People I met at school, particularly my wife, Barbara, and many of my pupils who remained my friends, do appear here, participating in the events and observations recorded.

After fifteen years in Wolverhampton I moved to a new school, Bishop Vesey's in Sutton Coldfield, teaching, as before, English and Art History, and from one village in South Staffordshire, Stonnall, to another, nearby one, Shenstone, settling there into my life with Barbara. Then, on my retirement from teaching in 1999, we moved to Suffolk, to Bramfield. We had been taking holidays nearby, mostly in Westleton and then in Wenhaston, for many years before we moved to live here, and I kept the journal continuously during those holidays. Other trips, to various places in France and Italy, in Wales and Scotland, and so on, make their contributions.

These journals have run alongside poetry that I have been publishing during the same period. This is not an accident. Sometimes the poems feed directly off the journals, but they have to do with experience in their own way, which is obviously not that of the journals. Nevertheless the specific detail of scene and event has been a necessary first consideration.

I could say that I thought of the journals as raw material, as description, to do with what Ruskin advocated as the prime necessity, that of seeing. Some poetics might scorn such business, some philosophy might decide it is a futile enterprise, but it lit up my life. Usually I would give myself a short time in the morning to write about the day before, if it seemed likely to be worth it, so the whole affair was necessarily impromptu. I did not often go and look something up. More recently I have allowed rather more ratiocination and reference into the observation, especially after having stopped teaching the sixth form, my favourite occupation, where I felt that the analysis was part of the spoken commerce of daily life, often the fresher for my not writing about it.

So to me these entries are vivid, because I was there, and because they have often played a part in my further thinking. As Roy Fisher says, about what he has seen and supposed, these 'have the quality of truth that I require'.

I owe thanks to many people, but let me mention in particular Sue Gregory and Andy Brewerton, who read some of the pile of closely written, hard-backed exercise books that comprise the journals so far, and were pleased by them, Julia Blackburn and Herman Makkink who took steps to encourage me to think of publication, Michael Schmidt, who began publishing extracts, most of them reprinted here, in the PN Review in November 2002, and has continued to do so ever since, and Tony Frazer who suggested this book and made it happen. And my family, of course, Barbara, who has always been reading and encouraging, and Ruth, and Eric, who also did a lot of checking of my text.

January 2006

17 October 1970

The eleventh tree is the ivy, in its flowering season, September 30th to October 27th, then on down through the guelder into the elder, if Graves is at all to be trusted. Ivy this morning, in sunlight, at Footherley, umbels of pale green clubs. Slow wasps crawl there with folded wings. One falls backwards and drops onto a lower leaf, climbing up again, tired. Earlier, in the track, it is so cold that dew is like seawater and there is the chilly smell of sweet rotting. Only one white gnat floats under that wall, but here, later, on the hedge, are the wasps and blue flies. Most wasps sit still, pumping the sections of their abdomens slightly in and out. They fall hard and fly little. The stream surface by the bridge is as difficult to make sense of as it always is, so I am content with this: the emerald weed is stroked out straight, and over it there are two patterns of ripples, a still one of broad troughs, blue and brown, conforming to basic features of the bottom below, maybe, then, passing over this, smaller busy ripples of the same colours, like wrinkled skin shifting along over a rib-cage. In an enclosed place in the bank, wire thin ripples fidget up and down over each other, twitching like the gnats. The bank, beyond the barbed wire which is slung across the water, is the finest autumn wreckage of all, poddled and stamped by cows, and then dusted with fallen willow leaves, each small, and curved like a paring. The whole is a garnished pudding, poddell, pudd. There is mist in spite of the pervasive sun, so that shadows don't etch, but spottle, like drops with a blur round them, onto banks under trees and onto house walls and barn walls. Things, which are thus not clear-cut, seem free to tug contexts around themselves. A spray of oak hangs below the dark canopy into the sun by the trunk. A rose in Keeper's Cottage garden pulls the barn wall and the cottage and all of the garden round it, where it catches the angled light, pink. Bracken fingers come through a holly hedge and make textual play with it. Acorns are sometimes steel cores inside a loose, ribbed, brown leather, dry skin. They fall as you walk under the oaks. The dog in the stream makes huge cups of yellow light, which swell from his black body in the centre of them, growing off him like round petals. The green ivy flowers come out of small, heart-shaped, fleshy leaves and these leaves have their own particular light green and a single, accurate line of wine red along the thickness of their edges, which colour also suffuses their stems. There are nineteen or twenty little knobkerries to each umbel. A wasp, passing in the air, burns lemon.

The leaves are wet with cold water. A man passing on a bicycle peddles more professionally as he gets closer, and smiles, though he doesn't look up, he keeps his eyes fixed on the spot just in front of his front wheel.

There is no euphonious bawdry about these wasps, never a hum to notice. Your words ought to be pale green, unmelting, and tough, like the colours the insects crawl amongst, quiet as the beginning of winter deaths. No Bacchanalia, in spite of the ivy coming after the vine, and both implying resurrection, he supposes, by their spiral growth. Hedera helix. I suppose the agaric is under the birches on the Chase. Here there are crab apples though, white-green, one nip of which would put bitter fur on all the teeth in your head and raw spit on your tongue. A broad-leaved plant is in the foreground, dashed in with emphatic light and dark, then the roughened field of grass runs off to a horizon of thin, grey hedge, stopping and starting along the rim. Dock to mist. Wan green, wan wasps, 'worn out with toil'. Gwan, feeble, faint. Win. Gain by labour or contest. Now there is little more to win. Suffer. Strive. Pale, pallid, fallow, pale brownish. 'His hewe was falwe'. Fealu. Pale red. Yellowish red.

30 November 1970

The dog's walk is in the dark now, darker tonight because of rain-cloud, though, of course, the sky is not at all black, but always blue, and whiter at the horizon, brightest towards Shenstone and over Spring Hill. The road surface is light, blueish I think, with trees standing up from the hedges and the dog melting into the bank, though clear enough in silhouette when on the open asphalt. Although things on the ground blur together, one is conscious that everywhere is a mess, after all the rain. Water is running full tilt somewhere in the wooded pits opposite New Barns Cottage, and again behind the hedge the other side of Primrose Cottage. Puddles widen from the verges and pool in the field gates. A stream comes down the left hand furrow of the track behind Stonnall House Farm, into the drain at the bottom. The air itself is thick and wet, so that there is steam coming out of your mouth when car headlights approach, although it is not at all cold.

Smells in the dark. Coming by Ivy Cottage there are first the lights in the windows illuminating the triangle of grass with the finger post on it, then a slight hint of bacon, which turns quickly into a nasty taste of smoke as if rubber were burning. Then there comes the sewage stink from the ditch opposite, still and insidious. Passing on the way back you get the sewage first, then a sudden, full scent of bathwater with salts in it, and the sound of water in a drain, and the shouts, then, of children upstairs, where the lights are on and the curtains drawn. Further along the lane the emptiness felt like death, but here it is completely humanised. Small, white moths are about, in numbers. John Smith's courtyard is lit from someone working in the big barn, and from the lamp on the house wall. Damp air like smoke. Green doors of stables with their lower halves closed. A big dog, in the orchard, barks as we pass and moves behind the holly hedge to keep close to us.

1 December 1970

An hour earlier today, thanks to a two period afternoon. Children in the garden at Ivy Cottage, hidden behind hedges, talking, the rank smoke from the chimney smelling like it did last night, fanning, turning down into the road, puffing through chinks below the chimney coping, pea-green against the blue sky from one side, grey from the other. The chimney is a leaking, gimcrack thing on one end of the house, the end where there are no curtains in the windows, as if one were to expect chickens inside on the windowsills, roosting, treading over each other, like there were in the house in Chesterfield which was once the Workhouse. What are they burning? Later, on the way back, there is a man painting the ceiling at the other, ivy-covered, domestic end of the house. Some late preparation for winter festivity. The sky is by Poussin in his most austere colours, pink cloud, slate blue in its crevices, on a duck-egg background. It is set over a light green field that looks as if it were spring. An old sort of fresh green. The soaking things have had has sopped them with one more richness. The verges are viridian, chrome yellow, though the roads between them are dry. That sort of balance. Pools are everywhere in the fields over the disused excavations that used to be brick-kilns, and big trees are toppling inside the swamped wood. A young man is walking slowly past the end of Hook Lane, wearing some blue coarse-cloth jacket. He is thoughtful. You could believe that he was still a countryman, despite the sulphur lights of the main road in the pearl grey bed of distance behind the near fields.

11

The Manor of Shenstone, four miles from Tamworth, containing ten carucates of land, enclosed park three miles in circuit, other woods without number, with we know not how many tenants, freehold and bond... a mill that goes by water and which could be leased for ten pounds, rights of free harvesting, several rivers full of fish flowing among the lands and amounting in all to six miles and more... (petition of Robert de Grendon to the King, 1333-5, for restitution of the enumerated lands which had been owned by his father Rauf de Grendon).

11 December 1970

Friday. Detention duty. Late back. All the walk in the dark, and, when I was crossing the field past Grove Hill, I turned up the side of the hedge, through the cabbages, out on to the small knoll itself. The place is exposed on all sides from below. It is the navel of the area. East is the black clump of trees in Thornes churchyard, one field away. North, the whole sweep of Stonnall, a bed of lights, clear away to Lynn and, on the horizon, Wall, at least. West, the hill slopes more savagely than I expected, down to the Chester Road, which is full of heavy traffic, with the garage to the left making the brightest glare. Opposite, over the road, the bulk of Castle Hill, with the lights poured round its base, and, more thinly, up its side. The Chester Road is hidden there by Fishpond Woods. The living places are more or less where they would have been in the Iron Age, I guess, under the hill fort with the main North-South track-way along the valley, avoiding the higher, clayey, wooded slopes over there, along the edge of the Bunter formations stretching south to Birmingham. The tree on the top of this knoll is... what? Stunted, anyway. There is a sort of bunker round it, as if someone had attempted some perfunctory excavation. Looking for evidence of a sacred place. Looking for the grave of the White Knight. There must have been an Iron Age post here, fronting Castle Old Fort across the road. The bunker could be a World War Two affair? Did the Home Guard ever use such places, to command the road in the ancient way? I brought a handful of dead leaves out of the depression to identify them, and the tree is a beech.

25 December 1970

Yesterday was frozen all day. There was the sound of heavy traffic far off on the Chester Road, hollow, like the noise bouncing inside hard, inflated tyres. Snow began in the afternoon, in small bit pills, then mingled into softer lace flakes putting the sugar on the fields. Today, the snow re-began early, cunningly. Not much traffic, only two cars along Gravelly Lane. No sound of the snow except when you stand by bits of the hedge where oak leaves are thick, golden fawn, dry as chapattis, and broken like them, rather than torn, at their edges. Here the flakes rattle slightly. This quiet. The wide fields in the Boshes, beyond Cock Heath, have the finest gradations of colour, from white, through pea-green, very light, under the fringe of the wood. The trees fade as if in deepening mist, each keeping a clear fan shape, however. The hedge swerves and writhes away. All blues are killed, even in the asphalt where they are replaced in the bays, shelters, coves, where the road is bare because it is under some cover, by charcoals. The rose-reds and quiet oranges lose nothing and, in fact, take on more, by the removal of the blues. Shapes of houses are more cubed now that horizontals are carrying snow. The sun is white, like a moon, with no glare, round, and astonishingly crossed fast by a skelter of broken puffs of cloud like snow, in waves, high up. It is like a porthole into a storm, or the moon in a tempest, oddly at variance with the absolute impassivity of the wide landscape below. Birds are walking, or standing, waiting for something, in groups in low places. Rooks or starlings. The Grove Hill field is full of tall sprouts, with big heads as umbrellas piled with snow, but each sprout with a necklace of yellow leaves hanging sheltered beneath, wilting down round the stalk, which is knobbed with tight sprout balls. So the white field has a universal undertow of yellow, hidden, till you look for it, by the shining white tops. The underwings of a moth.

And yesterday, as I passed Footherley Hall, Christ the King's Home for Ladies, where normally one sees nobody, and it is just a country house with stables, water meadows, rows of poplars, a fine beech plantation, all rather lonely, there were, as dusk came, families visiting for Christmas. The front door was open, and two nuns were shouting cheerfully to a boy. They wrestled a little with him, as he was leaving with his parents down the front path, one nun bouncing him up and down, holding him under his armpits.

The nuns, black and white, in the snow. Then, framed in the door, a sister all in white, speaking. And one more nun, away to the right of the lawn, her headgear tied up, rather like a towel or a cook's hat, a mixture of church and kitchen. She was pulling at the twigs on a holly bush and calling back excitedly, head tilted up, to the others. Not in English. In Spanish I suppose. Fetched from Spain to look after the old ladies who were hidden inside now they had been visited. In Christmas Eve snow. In this far-away place.

20 January 1971

Back home at 6.45 after rehearsal from 3. Darkening fast. No stars. Featureless, opalescent sky, warming a little to the north and with a white, static blaze over Shenstone. Only three cars pass me in the lanes during the whole walk, which takes an hour and a quarter. Not much wind, but the corrugated roof of the shed outside John Smith's creaks uneasily in groups of three sounds, two or three times as I pass. Lights in windows cast shadows and New Barns Farm sends the hedge across the road so that the dog flickers through. Away from the lights, in the even gloom, he worms along as a thick clot in the centre of a sleek, rippling penumbra, the metal on his collar sounding strangely harsh out of the liquid impression, and, when he ducks suddenly up out of a dark crotch in the verge, where a ditch rises, out onto the plain grass, your eye both stays with the blot he comes out of, and goes with his shape, which is now smoother, wiped cleaner like after a plunge, so that he seems for a second to have walked out of himself, and there is a stutter as he catches up. The visual field is seeded all over with small, pale grit, so that, as you look at the road close ahead, you see that the pebbling is not on its surface but above it, between it and your eye. Then you find the same texturing over the verges, hedges and all darker forms. So one is looking through a medium, at objects which lose the denseness of themselves as a consequence, and an unlocated floating results. If you stare hard at the side of a telegraph pole its boundary is not there, even as a gradation from light to dark. There is no such steady, observable thing. Rather there is a line which you assume beneath a sequence of nibbling light blots, which move up and down as the eye moves, and a stalk of thick dark up the centre of the pole, which can send bulges and constrictions up and down its length, like a throat swallowing. Or the edges double themselves, the outer one a paler ghost, and, when this is so, the light patches pour in and fill between the two edges, as water, if you poured it on a polished tabletop with two scratches, close alongside each other, running across it, would run between the scratches, ending square at the top and the bottom. Back towards the streetlamps, there are two faint shadows of you, facing you on the glowing tangle of a bush. Next to them is the road-sign, LYNN, black on white metal, so bright that the sky behind it is darkened, and blotches of light drift over the black letters. A pad of privet stands up behind the sign, so multiple with tight shadowed leaves, so thickly detailed like this, that it feels heavy to the eye, and surprises it as a lump of lead would surprise the muscles of your arm if you took it up expecting steel or aluminium.

26 January 1971

Tuesday. Did not notice the volume of the rain until I arrived home. Then, into the dark, with an umbrella. The dome of sound this makes hooding the head, all the time the rain is on it, importunately, and under trees so heavy that the fabric bounces and the handle responds springily. Sounds are rising from your body, the hiss of your plastic coat, like a warning, difficult to localise because it circulates around under the canopy, mixing with sounds from outside. And smells, wood-smoke from Laurel Farm, where there is flickering firelight in a front room, traces of wood-smoke hanging here and there in the road. Bright white drops are on the ends of the spokes of the umbrella, and on its toggle. You see them ignite when the rim dips below the horizon. Then the spikes look clean and black when the rim tilts up against the sky. Car headlights approaching you make the blank road suddenly glitter with a crop of dashes and spikelets. There are fungoid blooms on walls. The different textures show more dramatically a bricked up door in a barn. Seaweed shapes reach up walls from their bases. There is some sort of lichen, matt now against the shiny skin of blue brick. In the track the running water is so fast that bits of froth almost keep pace with you, bucking over the hatched grooves of the mud.

August 1975

Between the houses and on up White's Lane, out towards the pale cornfields. Over beyond the darker cabbages there is a most bright window, low and unmoving. It comes closer as you move on, then it is a fire, left unattended. It is the butt of an old oak, roots frizzed, smothered with white powdered ashes, heaped in churned, soft earth. There is not much free flame, but short flips of lime and cobalt at the roots of the orange-white. The bellies of the logs have been converted to cells of burning, without losing their shape. Sprinklings of sparks puff. There is a tapping, like a finger on a drum-skin, or snaps, like bones giving way under thick flesh. The heat and the wood-smoke make a home under the hedge. Nobody comes, though this is a bigger bonfire than most could make for a celebration. A trunk, abruptly, rolls and it is a shock. You expect only men to make such decisive moves. A large can is positioned under the hawthorn, where, obviously, somebody was sitting. There are hours of burning left yet. There are voices from fields away, back in the village, and subdued traffic occasionally from the Blythburgh road.

At midnight, on the beach, there is again lime green, flickers of it, in the waves as they break. The green spurts lift in, or fall sideways, and repeat in the same places, so they may be jellyfish. No noise away from the shore, on the Green, after we come back and I sit on the front wall.

In the morning, the front tyre is flat, so into Halesworth, where the Market Square Garage turns out to be interested and fast, so that a new tyre is fitted within minutes. The others have gone for a walk and I have not brought a door-key with me. So I turn off, up lanes, to Bramfield. Now the skies thicken in muffles of grey and floating, fine white mizzle. But, inside the church, Nicolas Stone's statue of Lady Elizabeth seems content. The lips smile after a tyre well fixed. Alabaster clears to nearly glass. A thin oil seems to sparkle on her skin and clothes. There are bits of hard plaster fallen into the crooks of her elbows. Maybe I can smell bat droppings. The reflection of the coloured east window takes up changing shapes, slides and fixes over her surfaces. On the back of her hand it is white, picked out with red and blue, and again on the scoop down from her lower lip to her chin. A mullion splits the highlight on her cheek. On the polished pillow, a leaf of petrol spreads. She lies in a bed of crystal spikes, while the rest of the church lulls, moodily.

Suddenly, all the strips of lace about her catch my attention. Thick lace, cut with bold, packed patterns. Her double frill of collar, both layers trimmed in a seam of wheels and bars and flower-suns. Long cuffs, filled to their double rim with buckles and flowers, punched into the glassiness. Pipped and seeded shapes are strapped together, and the gaps between them tight with pellets or rays. Oppositions in sequences, and order picked out. Something that the mind can cope with on its own terms, like numbers stamped over the carved clothes, over the drapery which was cut while nobody counted anything, by hands and skill, straight from the eyes and touch and the grain of the stone and the temper of Caroline England, impossible to explain or even describe. Adjectives flutter. Broad strips of lace edge the robe, strong running curlicues of leaf, diamonds and squares running alongside. Down her body the bedspread is striped, once or twice, with the simplest, most open and satisfying pattern of all: flat basic shapes, stars crookedly set, split seed pods radiating unevenly from between petals or out of the ends of them, the chinks between the discs filled with waves and the waves joined by a thread or two, slight variety in the simplest systems. These inroads open up the stone like grills. They let shadow into the surface as they let mathematics into the sculpture. Rest in the tracks. Elsewhere the brilliant surface comes clear of everything you can say. The curdled matrix has the brown tint of dried oranges, or, softer than that, of caramel, or creamed coffee. That analogy makes its tour of the whole event showing some more of it. A spoon went through firm gelatine to make these creases. The nails on her squared fingertips are worn smooth, and the finger ends are peppered with glints as if they were sugared. The stone becomes food. Along the end of her pillow is one clear, thin zig. She smiles. You can count parts of the pattern on her lace. You can take such facts away with you easily. The car stands under the crinkle-crankle wall. Water falls filmily. Lunchtime on a Tuesday. Words will be left to make where you are now, and what you have seen. Stone kept account books and was almost illiterate, though his manual on fortification is stylish, and contains, I have heard, jokes. A single zig between ruled lines across the end of her pillow. The pillow is polished alabaster. Stained glass reflects on it, shaping up from where you stand, dodging about. It all has to do with the Lord Chief Justice, with his son, with Theophilia, Elizabeth, Winifred and their mother and father. You can remember names. White marble and black touch, imported across the North Sea. Facts. But how are the statues, and how is the invisible woman?

April 1977

So many dapper, smiling fears come pretending to be only entertainment. Ducking down and tilting their heads to get their faces closer to the children, or running nimbly after the girls, clattering a lower jaw. Which could be snapping or laughing. It could be applause at their own performance, recommending itself as all part of the dance, circling amongst the bystanders, sweeping up the shy and the poor, even an unsmiling girl dressed in black who was trying to walk past. It has no hands so it cannot accept any money that might have bought it off. So what can you say to its wooden, polished face? Ruth screams. It is a tall goat. You can see its painted white eyes and neat black horns. The only soft thing on it is a grey, cotton-wool goatee, glued to its chin. How loud and how dead a jaw it runs around with! The legs are those of a cricketer from the knees down, stitched with bells and wearing black shoes. It is taller than a man should be, and it looks across at you over the heads of the spectators and the stick dancers. For a moment or two there was an equally tall lion, with a shredded, golden mane. He did not look in this direction. Often the goat did, in his royal blue and gold coat. He stooped, to get down near the back of your neck, and danced only with his legs. He could see you clearly enough for his purposes, through his throat, and doubtless, since he was trained in Gloucestershire, and has come here along Will Kempe's route from London to, now, Attleborough, doubtless he knows what sort of smiling to expect.

What am I expecting to see at dusk, out past where the houses stop, where the human goat might walk? New categories. Sudden understandings, over the verge and under the scrub oak. So much of a fright that you resent the morris men. Listen to the steady, quiet quacking of the pairs of duck as they firmly cross the sky, mapping out their course. As they come down on water they are immediately so noisy that it is an outrage to the silent evening and your gentled blood, and I think your eyes widen. Certainly the concussion of flapping wings is an assault on the sides of your head. Where are north and south? The coast is miles away and the stars are hidden by branches. Hawthorn. The stream looks icy and immobile. White mercury. But it makes random, disjointed, urinous sounds. As the light goes there is an interim period when the pheasants, more of them than you could imagine, thrash their way out of trees. Moorhens, with voices too big for them, comment and walk into ditches. There is a network of water, down low, slipping everywhere. One thrush sings coherently, sure and composed, and one or two owls search and hoot in a dry, restrained manner, as if they were not using all of their breath. These are sweet violets in the orchard, wide in the dark. Celandine everywhere, wet yellow wax. Mats of purple dead nettle. Clear water, come here in winter and not yet churned by men's feet. Smell the garlic.

In the mornings there are pied wagtails, clean birds, with bills full of nesting material. They search the flint wall behind the curtains of ivy, and the barn roof, in the fresh sunlight. They stand for absolute certainty, with every feather a signature and each movement predictable. The purpose of them has been decided already. You can make a memorandum of it, as the White King said. The ivy has been scrupulously polished, every stem and leaf. Make a note of it so you cannot forget. Like this. Look. Viewed and valued and priced, by Edward Bedingfield, Gent, Thomas and Francis and Daniell, 17th February, 1629. In the parlor. Item. 'The picture of an Moore on horseback in a large Table the picture of Saint Jerome the picture of Mr. Coke his mother'. What are you looking at? A black man or Anne? There was an Anne here, says a footnote, the daughter of Richard of Stansted who married William Baker of Bury in 1561. So she was not far away. But there were also Saint Jerome and Bridget Paston. The two of these define your choice about what might be on the large Table. It was a list made to settle what was there. But it is a puzzle. Since he had the picture of a saint, he could have had a picture of 'an Moor' next to it. If he had a portrait of his wife, probably he had, next to it, one of 'Anne Moore'. Invent your punctuation and spelling. 'The Prologue is address'd. Let him approach'. Quince is doing it all the time.

At Gislingham church the plastic wad blocking the middle light of the south aisle west window, where the flycatchers and blue tits came in two years ago, is loose and lifts, and cracks down again with a quiver of metal and glass, at unpredictable intervals. The sound is hard and decisive, even bitter, in the quiet. In the Columbine Window I look also at the meadow saffron, which is white, with petals which could be just petals in general? The columbines, thunder-blue, are certainly columbines, however. You could list that. Some flowers are shown from above, excellent. Ah, but, other bits of the same blue are not flowers at all, but fragments fetched from somewhere else to make up the pattern.

The three-clawed, black cats' feet in the shield are unexpectedly grim. The outer pair of kings, headless, have robes so calm a green that they could be called jade, or celadon, like grass under an overcast sky. They promise peace and release and open weather later in the day. The royal blue cloth, Kate says, is cheap. But it is gorgeous in effect. The shed, erected at the back of the nave, at the tower end, is actually old, an elaborate gallery, varnished a raw, matt brown, and rotten. Nigel lifts the door away from its stairs, and climbs in to appear half way up in space, in the tower arch, wearing a filthy ARP warden's helmet. Dan takes him for a bogle. Which is funny. The children play with the hourglass dry depths of sandy dust under the floor of the back pews. The pulpit is a space ship, as last year. This year they talk to each other a lot. Dry as talcum. Rot has done its uttermost. It trickles. The ARP helmet floated ashore here somehow, from the war, which nobody here except myself lived in. Now we are in another cross-section of time. See them in their strange costumes, with long, untidy hair, Nigel unshaven and with round lensed spectacles. See how they let the children play in here. Listen as Dan asks what else happened to Christ, and Nigel suggests that they read the book when they get back. Brambles pile over the lower panes. Slow worms slide into motion. A sound from a mouth is as much an archaeological feature as the Jacobean altar rails, dried or drenched, as it comes out in the space under the roof beams. Touches will be left unwiped. Gestures of children must stay. How strong is stillness?

August 1979

Solus to the track at King's Farm. Looking for owls, but also looking for the way things handle, and, for this, it is necessary first to simply stand still, which is at once to sidestep the roles. Full light still. Pink cumulus heads look over flint-blue, low strata round the horizon. Rain over. Smells in suspension, solid and sweet. Along the edge of the field, where stubble has been ploughed in, a drift of smoke-blue mist. Patches of froth in the puddles in the track. Small flints crunch. The field is edged with hedge and bracken, under which is a hidden warren, obviously, as rabbits are out over the broken soil, lolloping. Binoculars see the ginger patch on the back of the head, behind the ears. The ears translucent like the corn stubble. The high eyes, big and set in bone. Tranquilly the dusk comes, soothing the air. Two blackbirds quibble and cluck. A robin sings. Grasshoppers begin, and keep it up, two of them, to my right, louder and closer. Bats twist. Pigeons make their moves. The sky yellows. The pink heads whiten. More silence. I am under an oak, and the leaves hang round, each curled, faded. Some eaten to the veins. Others just pierced. The doing of this is something over, and knowing how it was done, by... maybe, caterpillars, is like knowing a story. If I saw it being done... it would be like listening to a story, surprisingly pleasing to be being shown it, as it is now to watch a fly, in silhouette, moving round a twig. So separate and far a little event, I am only hearing about it. The trunk of the tree glows as it blurs in the darkness, so that, though it is close, it looks impossibly far. Just glimpsed, although the signs are I am looking steadily at something two feet away. Its base descends into bracken, which, I take it, shadows the trunk down there, a long way down, by my feet. Very, very gentle shadows. Amazingly unemphatic and gradual, and the bracken so still it must be behind glass. All this is indoors, to judge by the feel of it, and the smell, too, seems to have accumulated in a room. When wind comes, slightly, the curved twigs give a single jig, each its own way, perfunctorily—a gesture to show that they move like that, that twigs move like that, the account of how a wind might move them. Instead of coming closer to objects and events, I feel them move off further into fiction. Their establishment is due to a grip I have on them which comes, as I think this out, from a sense of sinus pressure at the inside of my eyebrows, either side of the root of my nose, and, if I push out my lower lip, from the tucked muscle under that. A warm control, which keeps anything chilly and immediately real away. The bent leaves are a sight I see. The furry 'trunk'. The white plates of water in 'puddles'. The spectral rabbits melting, repeating their excursions and retreats. My head has to be turned to see the different corners of the scene, which come in turn, then, not as if they were all there, all round, all the time. I scan all round, with the binoculars or without. The field of vision. Things behind the head are not there while they are not being recounted, but are recovered each time I look. Strictly memories. How briefly the sounds come above silence. In the leaves, a tapping, as of hard moths on dry paper. Sometimes in a run, like a single pebble. Reality is not possible, because immediately the noise is in the past, and one of a pair or more of fictions. A decisively heavy blow in the thicket, not followed by any consequence. Is there fruit to fall, or feet? Only possibilities are made by these sounds. I shift. A response of some sort, on the path, about five paces away. I need the binoculars to collect light enough the see even that far, and it is a… now I come to it… in bits… yes, a rabbit, rigid, looking, sitting, tense, quite clear. It relaxes, hops away slowly round the curve, past a puddle. The response, I work back to it, was its sudden jerk as I moved. Did I make it a rabbit by expecting it? Not so. I was not so primed. By now I don't even expect to walk back to the village. The world does continue to produce rabbits. They are features of something I am not making. But no more full of impact than events in a story, products of that decorum. To die would not be to see the world stripped of glosses then, however terrible or exhilarating that might be. It would be to read it from behind this block, this thick, warm, spectatorship, from this warm audience seat. Opening to the world… there is no such possibility. It would be easy to tell other stories about it, so that a demon appeared as objectively as the rabbit did—but pointless, since that fiction too would be a tale. My head would turn, and either side of the look would be the silence, and immediately before and after the sight, it would, as now, not be there. Walking through sentences. I hear this bit, then that. Already the rabbit is résumé. And, when I move, my heavy shoes will crunch. Others will hear and see. I shall knot and shrink, a snail clenching, and stop watching, and be a role, which, in another way, is a system of parts—feet walking down there, shoulders hung out at the sides, hunching, a collection with no discernible centre to consider and contact it from, know it from. Indeed the release will come when I just let myself out into it again, and, giving up knowing, just do it all again. Once again the absolute sighting of me, or of the rest, was not there, and, as Nigel reminds me, back in the sitting room, just as well, since that sort of given solves everything, and at once takes away the process in which we live and find any sort of responsibility, over 'seventy thousand fathoms of water'.

25 August 1979

Bob and I leave for a concert at Blythburgh: Gemigniani, Locatelli, J.S. Bach, Kodaly, Telemann. A harpsichord and cello. Never gave much thought to it before we got there. Arrived when the church was empty, and the low, warm, evening light coming in suffusions into the dryness of brick and stone. The spot-lit angel just visibly haloed. In some way you can be sure it will be beautiful. I feel like sitting at the back, so that the distilled air over the floor, the grey slabs, the clay and straw colours, the squads of bricks marching against each other at angles, the big shed, silver and blue standstill, will all be in front of us. But Bob chooses the second row. It fills with people. Millais blue dresses and black socks, precocious little girls with widely spaced eyes, interesting mothers, a blonde with escaping hair, a man with a rubber mouth all across his face, another man, this one with the blonde woman, in sandals, with half his moustache white. The jowelled, stuttering clergyman, in black, seeking for two unobtrusive Dutch people, who will need a lift back to Walberswick because they are counting on buses, which don't exist in this part of the world. Then the cellist, and within moments we find that he gasps, repeatedly, out of the side of his mouth. Yes. And looks a little shy and flushed. A fluff of newly washed, light hair, and going bald in a hidden coin, as he ducks. Gold glasses. Tight mouth. Slight accent, but richly edged voice, confident in tone. A big gold ring. Shining metal on his bow, on his finger. The cello spike on a plank. A barley sugar stemmed standard lamp with a lemon yellow shade and tassels. He is younger than I am by a lot. He is, within seconds, in complete control of everyone, and very passionately so. The cello rocks and seems to crack and bend. The hand drives down to deep notes, like killing things, then hauls them up alive and shouting over to the high strings. The acuity of contact between bow and string, where the tiniest contact has razor edges and a vast, open voice inside, parallels the enormous, liquid sunlight touching the dry stone pillars, desiccated white, absorbent, and the baked, cooled brick floor. But the still building is undone by the quite unbelievably curved music, which twists beyond any tracery in a few seconds, and the fingering hand makes more deft moves in a minute than the carver of a row of gargoyles, more than a mind thinking deeply could. The limping mind, which hovers, repeating thoughts to be sure of them, before moving on. The musician, feet drawn in, tap, slap on the grating floor, head turns aside, elbow and shoulder thrown in, frown, grimace, the calm gold spectacles and washed hair. No reflection. What, now, is fiction? He is not looking at anything out here, until the piece is over and then he focuses down the aisle with a slight flush at the fierce applause, a tight smile, and, I think, excitement, as he comes to Kodaly, goes behind the south, curtained bit of screen, returns alone, with, as he explains, the cello retuned, the strings loosened, notes deeper and richer chords all the time, a 'very passionate piece'. He smiles. The pause. Then the whole range. From slightest ticking, now solid as being hit, to sawing so fierce the bundle of bowstrings burns, threads break and flutter, he sweats. There is no blue and silver space now, but a golden brown body, a solitary, probably moving in a misty world. Anyway contact is immediate. Irritation is allowed and entertained with no compunctions. There is unabashed striking out into unhesitating tears, on romantic seashores, complete admission of death, howling, so quickly taken in control. A curve, a wobble, and it is a stamping dance not much less tragic, or blows, plucks, punching the streaming continuity, until it founders and the living is done by only plucking, itself taking up the main shape and carrying through lightning hands, back to the bow. How powerful it is that often the bow moves slowly, while so much happens at speed and volume, done by the lifted left hand. How enigmatic, anyway, at all, the littlest taps, indeed the whole indulgence, total appeal. The stiff, spread angels in the roof come back, like childhood friends, in the interval. Now the clean, electric light. The roof just out of focus. A bat come in through the open south door, maybe. Deep blue night outside. The high font a shining tower with children climbing round it. People pointing, talking about the bat, about, surprisingly, their lives and friends and getting home afterwards. Nothing afterwards to equal the Kodaly, though the Bach ends it with sweet interplay from Hester Agate. One is grateful for her short, firm stepping beyond. The cello. Alexander Baillie. Took the evening. Giving rein. Rain. Nights ago the rain on the lime tree in front of the cottage, in the dark. Like insects touching dry paper. All round me. Shapeless. Which ought to be heard. Then scrap all that. Take hold and ride and stamp and insist so thoroughly that the amazed attention of all the outside is on you, or withdraws, a little sulkily, to shiny blue night. Beyond the panes. Pains. 'Tap' go the drops, beyond pains. The painless drops. Nothing comes through. Gut and fibre cry, heckle and rage, joyfully. One journeying figure, flying through a plot of outrageous incident, at speed, sometimes with a quieter, whiter companion behind him, watching. Often alone and throwing every bit of furniture about, unsatisfied with the place. Then stop. Back come the angels' wingtips and faces and the clerestory windows full of floodlight, and their heads netted with up-thrown shadows of their panes. Rows. Like fleets of aircraft coming steadily on at the heads of vapour trails, far up, silent, coming rank on rank all the time, leaving music wrapped and heaving in a sack in your head, boned in, the splash subsiding in atmospherics in the ears, until you can pick up all the outside… a little, silvery noise of miles and miles, up to the stars. The stars are leaving, in little grasshopper noises, in puffs of mist, under the car wheels in the lane. One can always manage the falling cadence. A journal is a pile of such.

16 August 1980

Bats. People playing boules in a garden in the dusk, with the clink and clat of contacts. The church at Fussy, a simple Romanesque building, with six lime trees, cut back, touching each other and the church wall. Under them the round-headed side door, with no sculpture about it, just one line of white stone edging it. The door is closed. There is a car parked under the trees. Through the keyhole in the west door a light shows. I bend and look in. A man, with his back to me, is at the far end of the nave, standing facing the altar, possibly holding a book. He stays there for a long time. There is the small, round-headed window of the eastern apse over his head. Gold and white. A solitary man. Is he speaking? The car is still there half an hour later as Richard and I return from the lane, under tall trees, past water, over a level-crossing. Soft clouds in last light. All over Europe there are privacies, people on their own in specific settings, which they do not register as unique because they do not seem important enough to require any registration at all. There might be travellers who look through keyholes and then go before they are seen. He has been alone in the church. We took ownership of his solitude for a moment, and that mattered either more or less because he did not know it. Was he the priest? I assume so. Was he wearing vestments? In my memory he was, but I can tell that I am not sure about that. This was August 15th, 1980, last night, in the village outside Bourges. The trees are close to the walls. The boules click and there are shouts. It is too dark to play boules, you might think. On the slope up here there is the road between high house walls with barred windows in them, looking down into lighted rooms, deep and high, and there is a straw hat on a peg in some well-like hallway. Bright electrics. Dusty blank walls, and shutters, and our echoing footsteps.

We stay at the motel, with impeccably clean tiled floors and beds that are broad and have bolsters. The row of rooms is in the back courtyard, a stepped row of doors, each room with a bathroom tucked into it at the rear, with a shower and a cupboard, separated from the rest of the bedroom by a slanting wall.

9 January 1982

Thick snow all yesterday and last night. I seem to spend hours shovelling the light, foamy stuff, which powders in the wind and blows back on me, sticking to the hairs on my sweater. Wales took the brunt. Most roads there are impassable, so the Griffiths are cut off, we suppose. We are looking after their house, Ivy House, here in Shenstone, and their cat and their donkey. We open up the drive to Ivy House gates, wide enough for a car to get through, and make paths round the back to the kitchen door, and way out over the lawns, under the apple trees, clogged with lumps of snow, to the donkey's pen and hut, taking him a quarter bale of straw, stuffing his rack, piling his floor. He stands about and won't eat. The vet has been several times lately, and there is trouble with hooves. Snow up to our knees on the lawns, and drifts deeper than that. Roofs thick to the gutters. Icicles down from windowsills. Boys had to push my car up Boswell Road on Friday, at 2.50, on our early release. Main roads were covered, and traffic was slow. There are not many cars moving round the village today. The silence is padded. But no more snow falls.

I enter the deeper regions of Ivy House to check the house-plants. The central heating has broken down, but the pilot light and the motor keep the radiators just warm, so the chill is off. Joseph Reading, supposedly by Guercino, or even Rubens, looks cold in the snowlit front room. It's a big, hollow, vulnerable house, the oldest parts dating back to Henry the Eighth. The ceiling of the back kitchen is beaded with moisture, maybe condensation from the burner in there. Toby's cat-flap has let in half a bucket of snow in the corner. Barbara had to dig down to it from outside yesterday, to let him in. He has been sick in his blankets in the billiard room. I overfed him. He is on short rations and he might have worms.

The sky tonight is hard and clear and filling with stars, as we watch the eclipse of the moon. The shadow moved in from the lower left, the Sea of Fertility last to go, and the dark areas quietly lighting up rosy and soft, more and more, as the sharp blaze shrank and then went out. The disc was left full, like a softly burning quartz pebble, waxy, greasy even, lit from the edges in reflected light so that it was more obviously a globe than it usually is, and it seemed more in accord with its black background so you could sense the distance before it and particularly behind it, back through prickling stars. The seas were blue-grey as veins. In Macleods' kitchen the telescope was on the draining board, the window open, the electric light off, and the map of the moon was on the table. My binoculars gave a wider field. Now, as I write, back in our sitting-room, the moon is at the top of the window, lit three-quarters from below, the glowlight gone from it so it is just a weirdly angled crescent. Snow is not melting. The taps knock when we switch them off abruptly, so you have to be gentle, or climb up to pacify the ball-cock, in the tank in the roof, with your hand. The central heating works on. We phoned the Wheales, who were watching the eclipse, and Tim, Harry Kellett and Pat O'Shea, who were not. Ancient beliefs about the moon seem ludicrous. Its rotundity is so obvious even to the naked eye. This room is full of the sweetness of a white hyacinth, opened fully, and a blue one, half open. Strange, in the dark and with the window open to the icy black and white outside. The scent is filling the hall, and strikes you as you pass the front door. The moon is beyond smell, and now has only one small nibble out of its top. Moisture on glass. Barbara talks at length to Tim on the phone, about the Cambridge examination results. All three sections of the gas fire are steady orange, hissing, with the violet roots of the flames along their bases. Heat reaches me firmly, here in this chair. How often must the moon still have been visible when supposedly sucked out by dragon or wolf? Or were atmospheres thickened with volcano dust then? The Guardian surmised that this one would disappear into black, but the whole gentle berry was hung there throughout. 'I thought it looked queer', says one of the girls next door.

August 1982

How easy, in the electric light inside the cottage, with the windows so small, to forget the distance to the next house. Actually, no other buildings are visible from this one, and fields separate us from the one or two that are possibly somewhere near. Some shock in stepping outside the door, into the size of it. And surprise because—there is no wind at all. Clear night blue, some stars, a burst of crows cawing and moving out off the mountain, a bat or two, high or low, and an owl, very loud and close. Hard silhouette of the mountain. Small flies tickle. A drop falls in the water butt, which is now full. Small, pink clouds have left the sky to roll in the lap of Cader Idris. Stillness gets inside the holly. Here we are under the open Milky Way, under Vega, with the complete show, the Plough and Cassiopeia resting on the rim of our bowl, and one of the Perseids whipping silently to extinction towards the south east.

Pure postcard on Tuesday. Puffs of cloud overland, and thin cirrus over the sea. Hot enough in the wind to redden us all on Harlech beach. Into the dunes there, barefoot and careful for glass and harsh marram. A sudden glaucous blue patch, like litter, but it is cool sea-holly, tough and heavy. Rest harrow everywhere. Carline thistles, intricate, with glossy white-gold rays. Hollows floored with creeping willow, with catkins, and knotted pearlwort. The mashed urchin cases, chalky, broken, papery, in middens at the waterline. The leathery horseshoe prints, which are the eggs of the necklace shell, sunk in gleaming sand. A damp apple core, shoved into dry sand, with suggestions of sand in the teeth, grit in saliva, cut tongues, spit not thick enough. A crow opens and lifts off with a tilt from the wrack. Crab bits. Pin eyes. White legs. Closed claws. Flies swirl up and land on wrists, with offensive feet. Is there a smell of fish? Yet, also, there is a sudden sweetness in the air, or detected on the fingers. As you come out, the sea warms the backs of your calves. Soft, ropey weed wraps your knees. There is the immaculately displayed beach and hills, the picked out houses, grey and white, the neat, complete, strong charcoal grey castle on its diagonally layered rock, where Bran the Blessed feasted for seven years as a decapitated head, while the birds of Rhiannon sang, far out to sea, yet close in the ear, and no song was more beautiful than that, since it came from the other world, the paradise over the water, and could bring back the dead. Heavy water on me, as I stand out, up to the neck, compared to that. The sudden slap and rush over my head from behind, of a swell I did not anticipate. Chance and inadequacy. And the hundreds of people, to the right, along the beach. Completely a matter of no dream or final joy. Burnt skin. Greasy pink. Elastic and horny soles. Rubber shoes. A fat youth smacking a girl's legs with a yellow, plastic spade. Folding chairs in hands. Calves full of knotted veins. Loud voices which blemish the rush of water, and love between pieces of sandy meat. No repercussions out of the final air. Not so much a million, unseen relationships, as just a handful of responses. The ridges of the sand unexpectedly hard, banging the foot. The best mountains ringing us, reduced to glamour. Time should be a swift collection of light, clear empty glasses on a biscuit coloured shelf. The scent of the contents detached, adrift, somewhere a little way off, into which one might stumble, but it would be impossible to hold on or understand. Imagine the beach empty. The castle manned. The reduplicated houses gone. The empty shell of an urchin. Little, wafery skulls, which thought would darken and melt. Empty sockets, tilted to every corner of the sky. A sore neck touched by a ruggy shirt collar. Sticky hair. The breaks in sentences longer, this year. The eyes glazed in mid remark. The names vanish, and there is a yawn in the voice. What can string all this together?

10 August 1982

Diffwys fills the head of the valley, two miles up from where I sit against an outcrop above the junction of the Old Road to Harlech and the track to Tal y Bont. The Old Road goes to my left, between stone walls, as a field path. The Milestone, a slab on end, of Stuart date, has the names and distances on either side in old capital letters, shelled with lichen. Diffwys rises in a gentle shoulder from the direction in which the Road goes, and curves across, rising to a long ridge at its highest, where it comes out of grass and is ashy and umber, to the right. Then another low shoulder cups forward, enclosing that eastern side, too. Behind me I can see, over the nearer mountains and the estuary, all of Cader Idris. The Barmouth bridge and the open sea behind it, are to its right. The high fells and mountains beyond Dolgellau are inland, with a snatch of sunlight caught over there for most of the hour. There are tides of wind in the stone walls, which hiss in the small hawthorn hooking out of a low rock close to me. Grass heads fizz across the fields. My head is buffeted if I raise it above the rock. My hair and the short sleeves of my shirt are flapping anyway. Big humble bees swish past, carried, rising. I face Diffwys, the crest Tony and Geoff and I walked along twenty years ago, as we came up from Caegwian, over the next rise on down the track, where the valley is now a wood, as I know. Here I am alone, above the tree line. Isolated thorn bushes lean sideways, and mark out distances. The world is dominated by the concept of 'further'. I can hardly stop myself going on to the next vantage point. I desire to face further views. It is hard to sit still and contemplate. Out of the wind, between the head-high walls of the narrow tarmac road, which comes almost as far as this Milestone, it is warm. The trunks of ash and holly are bright. Leafage is open. A single sycamore looks black and shut into its foliage. Stones everywhere are whitened with lichen. Two miles of air give a silvery mistiness to Diffwys, which yet does not blur anything on it. The tilted valley is pierced by a river fringed with trees. There are black cows far away in the bigger open fields at the top, and a white scatter of sheep. A tractor, almost beyond my hearing, moves up there. There are a few houses and a caravan in a remote, sheltered meadow.

I realise that usually I assume that the world is full of thoughts, spaced out in the air, waiting for passing heads to entertain them. Here I feel a valley without thoughts, and thus the effort and futility of a small head pushing out ideas it has to make for itself. Any thoughts there were would stop with the removal of the head. There is no broad smile implicit in this scene. But it is certainly firm and clarified and out of the woods. It is definitely very serious. 'Hafod-uchaf', summer pasture, is the highest farm up there, then building runs out. The walls of the Old Road are neat, their coping stones laid across giving a rim of shadow, an edge with a direction. Then things fritter away into the smooth flanks. The valley is labelled 'Hirgwm' on maps, and joins the Afon Cwm-llechen below. Is that the 'valley of stones'? Near where I am sitting there was an old fort or settlement. Eyes have looked, and then stopped looking.

On the way up, near the Viga bridge, behind an area of broken stone where fires had been lit recently, under trees in a recess, there was a bed of tall hemp agrimony, with spearmint, meadowsweet, bees, hover flies, and the site was over-ruled by a gold, black and blue dragonfly, burring and swinging round, its speed out of all scale with the rest, its mobility from a superior order of gifts. There is nothing like it up here, nothing with that glare and expert attack. Nothing so decisively vicious, with immediate intent. Here the bees are blown about, and crows wobble low by the waterside. Dry gorse stems knock like sticks. I came up through zones, wood smoke by a farm, dung smells by a fold full of sheep, through woods with Melampyrum and fern, over the river in its gorge, where two men were panning for gold, their scintillant round pan down in the dark, crashing river bed. Up past the telephone box, a clump of overgrown corn sowthistle smothered in hairs tipped with glands and with the bases of its leaves curled back round its stems, then sheepsbit, then harebells. The rusted roof of a barn was the brightest item. There was a car parked at the end of the tarmac, with a dachshund whining in it. A headscarf was bobbing down behind a wall, belonging to a talkative woman who had left the car, hours ago, and walked up the Old Road and up the ridge to the summit. She was glad to have done it. Wouldn't stay because the cloud might come in. She drives away, shouting directions. That need for getting further up and seeing more, however worried the dog might be. I will get a good blowing up there, she tells me. Whatever is important, one senses, is up here. The lower regions seem like antechambers, full of distractions. Emptiness is, I now see this, the real goal. Above the vaults of eikasia. But today I turn back down to Gelli Rhudd.

11 August 1982

Today I begin to expect to see the person who just went round the rock. This region is Ardudwy, and across it, half way down, is the spur branching east of its main backbone down to the headland above Barmouth, and, south, off this spur, which contains Diffwys and Y Garn, run streams to the Mawddach, each in a valley, 'pleasant, sunny valleys', Cwm Sylfaen, Hirgwm, Cwm Mynach and so on. Dyffryn Ardudwy is not a valley, but rather 'good land', the western side of the backbone, between it and the coast, reaching up to the Llethr Ridge. This area was settled in the Neolithic, Bronze Age and Iron Age, like nowhere else this side of the Irish Sea except Salisbury Plain. Is this where I am? The Old Road I was on yesterday climbs up onto it, and so does the Tal y Bont track as it crosses the tops of the valleys. The Lost Cantref, the Hundred of the Sea Floor, must be off the coast, a folk memory of the Old People of Hengwm. So much I had better believe. Such talk gives you a strong sense of many hearts. What I felt yesterday, so much left to myself, was, perhaps, the loss of so many hearts. All the heads gone away, and so an extraordinary degree of emptiness. Anyway, in these lower places, this afternoon, there are staged scenes, presentations, enclosures. An isolated tree here must have a history, maybe even some power left about it. There is a knoll, an outcrop, and a rowan at a corner. You have attained an open space and in the midst of it there is a tall tree and under that a fountain and by the fountain a marble slab with a silver bowl attached to it by a silver chain. It is here that you find a this, by a that, amidst a where, and the place is full of dragons. The emptiness is possibly imminent, but, first, is the encounter with the man who has one eye, black skin and an iron club. He is the Master of Animals. You need to ask him for directions. Does this path join…? You catch his answers in the corner of your eye as the arm of a green branch, the wrist of a twig.

Against the chocolate heather a buzzard is bright. The heart leaves of the mullein are beaded with white, cold water, while elsewhere is dry. The drops don't soak in, but they stick to the felt. If it were not for the chill, an animal sweat would be suggested. The clump of trees at the top of the dell above the path is pine, oak and larch in a short row, a backcloth. A dead tree looks like a lightning flash, so bleached compared with everything else. It is on a mound. I climb up the slope and there is a wall, which was part of a house. It is roofless, with the fireplace collapsed in a tumble half filling the floor. There is a window in the gable, so they had an upstairs. A small window is next to the fireplace, and two recesses, which could have been cupboards or ovens. There are wooden sills, riddled and white, which a fingernail can cut into. The view from the gable end windows was the estuary, over the woods. The stream runs a few feet from the door. Sycamores have grown close and there is a hawthorn against the end wall. Two more fields are above all this, before you come to the open heather and gorse. Against the last wall is a stone shed, with no roof, but with a dead sheep inside it. There are also two strange stacks of stones, each of them over head high, both rectangular, about eight yards by three, built carefully as containers with rubble infilling. A green lane, now thick with nettles and rushes, runs to the farm. There are mossy rocks in walls, so big that half a dozen men could hardly lift them. An oyster shell is in a crack under the lintel in the main door.

Yellow on the flanks of Diffwys, between the umber and the ash scree. Old fields. Hafod, the summer pasture. Transhumance from the middle ages until enclosures in the late eighteenth century. Cattle for the English market. The permanent farmstead lower, the hendref, bottom land.

An elephant hawk caterpillar crosses the metalled track. It has pink eyes and is stiffly flaccid, like a slug.

There must have been moments when the people left these abandoned houses for the last time. Did they shut the door and go? Or come back to take the window frames, doors and roofs? Did they move out in summer? Did they keep them going for sporadic visits or in case they needed the higher pastures again?

There is a plastic motorway café knife, some cans, a bottletop.

Such fine walls, with those long slabs, four or five feet long, spaced at intervals, topped by a row of boulders.

5 July 1984

9 pm. The shine has gone out. The level lawn is scurfed brown. All round it are leaves. Rhododendron leaves are hard, sharp and pricked, with paler green whorls at the end of the shoots. Lilac curls up its tips, suavely. Hawthorn is hung down, tired and filled with a spatter of dead brown blossom. Forsythia spurts. Leylandii tower shaggy columns. Elecampane leaves crinkle. Rue is whiter, with slight yellow flowers and bluer foliage. The red-brown apple tree is nearest the house, dark in its hollows. Twists of mountain ash lurch out horizontally, cocked and fringed. Bits of yellow cinquefoil petals have spilled in a pile. The ruddy brick of the house is more than three-quarters hidden. The brown roof rises clear to the orange chimney, tinged rose by the sunlight that still reaches it. There is a thin spread of mackerel cloud all over the blue evening sky. Martins are flying, black backed and rosy chested. They float and flicker. The spinning clouds of flies have gone. Red and orange roses are in bud. There are foxgloves under a birch and their colour is saturated. All colours are saturated because this is all in the afterglow. Hawthorn blossom has fallen on the grass, like crumbled bread. Fallen lilac leaves are lemon. Blackbirds move. And people. Geoff's shirt shines between trees, and there is the click of Janet's shears. Phil's voice. He alone has seen me sitting here, and looks across. Zillions of leaves do not move at all. The one line of telephone cable strings straight up the garden in mid air. Blue comes into the brown roof tiles, and pink. Barbara is inside, teaching Charlotte. Both children are in bed, in the two front bedrooms, windows and curtains open. The blackbird comes jumping again, pausing

to examine, knocking leaves as he ducks under a bush. People are about in their front gardens. There is traffic in the distance, but the Croft itself is quiet, with blue-grey tarmac and low brick walls. I sit at the far end of the lawn, facing the house, come here to read since the inside is occupied and the outside is a massive inside this evening. There is a week of term to go, the examinations are over, the fifth and sixth forms have left. The Lichfield Festival begins tomorrow with concerts of Indian music and Mozart. Shears do more snapping. Geoff sounds as if he is digging. The sun has gone from the roof. No cloud now, and no martins. There are moths, jigging. I sense that the rhododendron has clenched its whorls. This is suburbia. I have been living here while most of this vegetation grew, for over ten years, never really conceiving it to be somewhere we would stop, but now at home here, knowing the noises, knowing there are fewer martins this time round. Fifty million people live, at the moment, in England and Wales. The all-time total of people who have lived anywhere is said to be 60,000,000,012. One sort of joke or another.

16 August 1985

Friday is begun under more purposeful rain, so we shop in Yoxford and get money from the bank in Saxmundham, then spend most of the day drawing in Dennington. I had arranged to meet Jeremy in Westhall at 6. I drive over, and there is no sun, no shadows over the road, everything chilly in itself, no show being put on. Puddles stretch across the minor roads, so I slow to a glide, with the brakes lightly applied. The rest of the time the water hisses off the tyres or warns me by jumping and slapping the underside of the car. A pheasant steps into the hedge. Always some bird or animal seems to put in an appearance as you approach, as if the roads were watched. I pull up outside the church and Jeremy stops alongside before I can get out, at 6 exactly, and the rain is over, the clouds thinned.

There is a watery sun, the air is clean, thoroughly washed, the gutters are running and dropping broken threads of drips, one of which smacks down inside the pipe from the 'valley' where the two thatched roofs, of nave and aisle, meet. That is where the leaks are. There is a thin moat all round the concrete ditch in the footings. The red stems and the pink flowers of herb

Robert are thriving there. We don't go inside at once, but circle round the building. Nobody is in the bungalow opposite, and the children are all inside at Church Cottages. No noises except of water. You step high in the thick, wet grass. The field below has been cropped, and it exudes some sweetness, which mixes with the smell of nettles. A Cropmaster combine is parked, light green, white and grey, in the field. There is some greening of the thatch on the nave and some slipping tiles on the chancel roof, otherwise the outside looks intact, though we know it is not. Irregular breaks in the high guttering are still shedding the day's rain. The south door is locked so we ask at the white house up the lane and are told that the far Church Cottage is where the caretaker lives. She keeps the key. Up the path there are sheep, which watch us. We puzzle over which doors are functional, knock on the wrong one, and a man comes into the back yard to send us round to another. She comes at once. She had locked the church early, not expecting anyone on a rainy day. Scaffolding should have been erected by now, but he has gone on holiday. There are no services until the repairs are done. The lack of company is breaking her heart. She depended on the company. Her husband said it should have been reed thatch and that the lead in the 'valley' was poor quality. This is the woman I have met several times, over the years, once or twice with her husband, then more recently alone, locking up, telling us of Dilly the goat and the Black Death. She gives us the key to the chancel door, and her front path leads directly to it, beside an orchard, then under churchyard trees. Inside, with the smooth turn of the little key. Inside for the next three hours, so that the woman comes to see, with the excuse that she wants to pick up a magazine. She suggests that she takes the key and leaves us to slam the door behind us when we go. She speaks to us from outside the door, partly hidden behind the red curtain that is hung over it, and finally turns away, stooping in her mackintosh, forgetting her excuse.

Intense silence all the time, growing more intense as birds quieten. We stand in various places for long periods, saying nothing. Jeremy folds his arms. He is dark and tall, sometimes nearby, sometimes away in a corner, doubled by a shadow. We look at the detail, checking what we have seen before, almost systematically. The wooden brackets protruding from the pulpit, a fantastic elephant, a man, a bird-man and an eagle. No lion. A series of inventions on exaggerated beaks and noses, rather than the four evangelists. The quality of the drapery of the figures on the seven-sacrament font, where they have not been smashed. A lady's dress in simple, elegant folds. A sleeve turned back to show its lining, painted green. The gesso stars, gold in a blue sky. The terre vert grounds. The stamped gesso saints on the pilasters that divide the scenes, their niches still darkened with colour, where the rest is more chalky and scraped. Nobody has ever picked at them, poked at the gesso, which would easily come off. Nobody has handled the font much since the great blows gouged it. Someone once pencilled a face where features had been sliced away, a childish trick of two eyes and a smiling mouth. That has been here for years. The angels supporting the bowl are faceless too, but one holds a rod and another crossed flails. Smatterings of the old colours have been left intact. The font stands tall, signalling its loneliness, the sophistication of its making, what it used to be like proved by the fragments that have lasted. There has been a quietness, one might say, of those who have been coming here for centuries and have been leaving it alone.

Watery, silvered sun puts its huge print on the north wall, past the door, touching the Christopher and stretching to the chancel arch. It contains the slanted shadow pattern of mullions, tracery and leading, and a branch of leaves, the leaves alone moving, making a specific, confiding wink, turning into a sheaf of blurred threads, then clarifying again. The texture of the wall, cross-lit, is fetched out. It is never smooth, but patched, puddled, smeared, worked over often, patted down, with dents refilled. The wall painting is on a darker, lower layer of plaster, and you can see the straight raised ridge above the figures where the newer plaster was applied. That ridge, too, casts its shadow under this raking illumination. Very pale red paint. The horned head of Moses, with God handing him the stone book of the commandments. These are now moving into shadow. The long, gleaming patch of sunlight travels to the wall beyond them. It is joyful after the dull, windy day.

There are no mats on the ledger stones, most of which are tilted, chipped or cracked, and set into pale bricks. The green glass in the chancel tinges everything up there, and, in front of that green, the pale bricks, the whole nave and the arcade react and flush pink. The Victorian pine benches are stained dark brown, but spotted white where their varnish has been taken off by whatever has fallen on them from the roof. The low light catches their rims, which shine along their backs and arms. Their hidden seats are the thick oak, never replaced, glassy with use, but you have to go and look closer to see that. By the second bench from the front in the Bohun aisle there is a bucket on the floor, below the patch of green slime up at the roof, and the chewed-off, black wall post. Water is dripping, sporadically, plink, high-pitched, loud, surprising the silence. The drops sometimes hit the side of the bucket with a crack which jumps you, because it is not watery. Occasionally, two drops sound almost together. The sound of the drip when it lands in the water is mineral and ringing. It cuts through the sound of your blood in your ears, opening the space of the church into an emptiness, which your blood might otherwise have clogged with its muffled hum. Stone floors flatten and bench ends rear in that emptiness. My heels begin to hurt and my feet fix where they are, so that I can't imagine being able to unstick them. My hands in my pockets grow huge, furry, gloved, swollen and glowing hot. I feel my sinus tight, my front teeth, where they are entering the gum, pressing. The tendons at the back of my ankles are hard as bone. There is a click, as some portion of my intestine loosens. I need to swallow, in bursts, very audibly.

The sunscape has reached the chancel screen, so its gothic arches and the tracery in them, over the painted saints, show their gold. One, stray patch of soft light is up in the roof, on a beam, as if indicating where the secret is to be found. The point of it all, very mildly suggested. The church fills with attention. My feet send out lines from my toes, not quite straight ahead, because I am locked into this stance, pigeon toed. These lines relate to the perspective of the sides of the benches, the run of the purlins and the roof beam. My verticality locks into that of the pillars in the arcade... Suddenly the ogee top of each reticulation in the tracery of the east window is gripping my head rigid. Fantasy blooms. A mullion on a nave north window, against the blue-white sky, has a large chip out of it. The top of the chip is straight and horizontal, the side of it slopes out and down. An open mouth, with a straight, short upper jaw and a long, hanging lower jaw. A sarcastic, open-mouthed laugh. The next mullion has a smaller chip out of it. A pursed mouth. All expressions are of some degree of astonishment. All of them are, more or less guardedly, critical. A shadow on an irregularity of the wall, immediately over the chancel arch, becomes a frown of concentration, as the wall becomes forehead. Everything upright is waiting. Everything horizontal stays where it is. There is no rhythm. The walls have stepped forward and are here. There is a double shadow on the whitewash behind each poppy-head in the Bohun aisle. Trinities, says Jeremy. But no more flames come in, and without them, the walls around have joined up and squared the place. The three roofs, the chancel one, single beam, massive, the nave and Bohun aisle ones, with purlins and wall plates, seal into a unity, gather together overhead. Things speak as emblems, as eidetic images, as persons, as styles. The west window, cut out in pure black now, has geometric tracery, quatrefoils, also two bare, straight transoms rather brutal in the side lights. So it is strong and unsubtle, and you could date it, if you felt it was coming too much to life.

And, lastly, things speak as things. I lever a brick up out of the floor of the Bohun aisle. There is golden sand under it. The brick is pink and white, and quite new. A brick.

As we drive out, I see, in my mirror, Jeremy's car hitting the puddles, the splash in his headlights, the shapes of reflected light contorting across the undersides of the canopies of the trees.

23 August 1986

It seems that not many people come into Malkin's Coppice. It stands away from the roads and the approach is up the private drive of the houses alongside the Pumping Station. You hop over the iron gate on the left and, what makes that slightly easier, is that someone has been tipping garden rubbish over there, so that there is a platform of this to step down onto. Then, at once, a wood, a thicket, with bramble near the light at the edge, then, in a pace or two, bracken, head high, under trees. And now there are only small clearings to let the light in. Birch, oak and mountain-ash. Birch stumps, still standing, with that hard, white bracket fungus, Piptoporus, much in evidence on them. There are many fallen logs below the bracken. On them the bark is a loose casing, still leathery, with the wood under it often a pulp of fibre. The ground is mulch, dry on its surface, then dark and squelchy underneath, so that, in kneeling on it, your trousers soak up cold blots of moisture. The bracken is heavy and strong, hard stemmed, switches you have to swing aside. Mosquitoes are wispy, blurred, searching the back of your legs to bite. I pick one out of the air with my forefinger and thumb. It is as if they are inexperienced in here, not having seen many men. They come thoughtfully, rather obsessed, and not expecting retaliation. They trust that they have their rights. And it is 'in here'. Voices come from the houses, belonging originally to the Water Company's employees, from 'outside'. Someone is cutting a verge with a strimmer. A car pulls away to come back an hour later. Some traffic is often on Lynn Lane, a field away. The factories are visible, through foliage, on that north side. But you are hidden by bracken almost at once. In the whole afternoon I do not get far, just a hundred yards or so, checking the spiders, which is the task I have given myself on this little, private raid on reality. 'Think, in this connection, how odd is the use of a person's name to call him!'

I have the book in the binoculars' case, which is slung on my shoulder, and keeps on slipping round and falling off if I bend forwards. It is quite an old book now, soft backed and beginning to take on a permanent bend, so that it is harder to flip through it, the pages don't spring back after your thumb. There is always the problem of spiderlings, too, which are not, of course, illustrated, so that what I can't identify, I tend to assume is immature, not photographed here, and smaller than the given dimensions. I have seen these minute Clubionids before. They have a lovely lucent orange abdomen. Their cephalothorax and legs as clear as water. They have black eyes, with the centre, upper pair wide spaced. I find two, but they do not answer any of my calls. Further in, on a smooth, green mountain-ash trunk, two very active spiders avoid me by darting round to the other side. I catch the one that lets me do so, the lighter one. It is a male. The only spider that I expect, because it moves like that and in such places, is Drapetisca socialis. This is nothing like it because this is almost all black. Then it occurs to me that if you imagine all the marks on the one illustrated as if they were somehow swollen, and spreading out until they almost met, the dashes alongside the roots of the legs fattened and so on, it might be… I imagine that, and there is that flicker of recognition. This is the melanistic form, assumed, it says, to be in industrial areas. I know there are doubts about how these melanistic specimens come about, how they are selected. But this is one, sure enough. What a pleasure it is, just now, to know that and see it, here in the wood where things might have no names! There are many Lepthyphantes. I keep turning them up. All are hard to distinguish this afternoon, because they seem to mix the criteria of the different species. The last one I find is bigger, the biggest so far, bright yellow on the cephalothorax, black rimmed, with a central line running up towards the back of the eyes then broadening. Abdomen with blotches and lines. I leave the wood aware that I am missing something obvious, then, at home, see that it was Labulla thoracica and I should have checked under the spinners for the three spots. This, under a log, where the springtails whizz, tiny glittering flies creep and waxy apricot-coloured centipedes thrash as you uncover them, is a Tegenaria, though small and far from a house wall or a shed. Silvestris. Just so. Small, neat and with the correct pattern on the sternum.

An owl hoots thoughtfully over to the east. I begin to find it worrying when I make any noise at all, and try to avoid twigs. I do not want anyone else to come in here and find me. But to move you have to put your feet down blindly, under the bracken, into the yielding ground layer.

Call out for sharp detail. The frizz of black bristles on the back of the palps of Drapetisca. These things emerge, definite, from the confusions. There was the fork mark, however thickened, on the head. The detritus is of old leaves, stems, twigs, moss and seed cases, a chocolate pulp, sticky to your fingers. There are the berries of rowan. There is an orange cartridge case. There is my own footprint from where I went before, and I recognize the tree I stood by when I made it. Bracken rends as I force through, impatient at unknitting it. The owl murmurs its hoot again.

Back in the living room with rain now plopping and knocking on the sill, I notice a small, pale spider moving steadily, high up, across the wallpaper by the curtain pelmet. He makes a spurt to escape but I have him in my plastic tube. In there he does not stop moving, he fingers the tube all round inside, laying his thread behind him. He is so small he can almost squeeze up alongside the cork. Male. Orange. Clump of white-green glinting eyes: Oonops domesticus. His legs keep working gently, as if he had been wound up. The eyes flicker as the head turns. The abdomen is darker than the cephalothorax, the opposite of what the book says, but that is because it is covered with long, thin black hairs. Bristowe says this spider makes smooth, groping progress without pausing or changing direction, so that you can tell it across a room by its movement. It would move up to a fly with the same, unexcited, soothing motion. Words come true. I loose him in the lobby, on the whitewashed wall, where the electric light throws his angled shadow in front of him, more hunched and ominous than he is, and catches each of his hair-thin feet with a corresponding hair-thin shadow foot, step by step, as he descends on the craters and floes of the brick.

'"What do you call yourself?" the Fawn said at last. Such a soft, sweet voice it had!'

30 August 1986

Professor Biddle has an open evening at Repton, and Ailsa and Richard arrive in the afternoon, so we pile into their Peugeot and drive up. The main street is already full, and through traffic is impeded. Last year there were three hundred people. This year must triple that. We are split into parties, each conducted by a marshal waving a red and white pole. Professor Biddle stands out in the dig, on the mausoleum site, and his voice rings out in the darkening air. Students crouch, scraping at the oddly shaped graves exposed round the edge of the site, with loose tape measures snaking, and plumb lines and awkwardly balanced metal grids. Hundreds of labels are pinned to the sides of the trenches. The cut red sandstone of the Saxon mausoleum is exposed at the bottom of the shallow, central rectangle. The Vikings took this structure down and buried their chieftain on top of it, in the rough rocks we now see cleared further back. He was surrounded by his 120 dismembered followers who had died of dysentery and influenza in the winter of 873. Outside this area the graves are of Danelaw notables from subsequent years. Gold cuffs have been found. All this, in the vicarage garden, will be covered up again this year. Our party stands around in a half circle, several persons deep. A still evening. A silent crowd. For us this was rather an impromptu visit, and it has caught a significant moment, a rare opportunity, all the more moving because of the unanticipated number of those interested, their intense involvement, and the fact that we are all here in the evening. There are a lot of dead people here. They have been dead long enough not to be corpses, but what is known about them puts them here, in this garden, suffering from influenza. This gathering of the living has come to something of an occasion, expecting insights.

North of the chancel of the church we hear Mrs Biddle discourse on the burials here. The cranium of a skull stands out of a vertical bank. Arm bones protrude either side of it. Is this some sort of a show? Can one quite believe it? A jawbone lies askew on top of the pile of soil. A complete Viking has been found here in these last few weeks, hence the newspaper reports. Hence, of course, the crowd. He had his sword, and a silver Thor's hammer hanging round his neck. Miolnir. Did he speak that word? No sound of it, or sight of him, at the moment, however. Plastic sheets cover semi-circular frames, as if they were protecting vegetables. Only the bottoms of trenches are sludgy. We troop away, squeezing past other groups, feeling anxious to get to the front, but conscious of those behind. We pass through the gate of the headmaster's garden, and, in the dusk now, climb a steep, loose spoil heap and take our stand in rows on it as if we were the audience at an amphitheatre, hundreds of us, adults and children, cheery talkers, loving couples, solitary thinkers. At the front a length of string runs along the edge of the great pit into which the ground falls away very steeply. This is thought to be the Viking dry dock, let into the south bank of the Trent, which at that time ran behind that wall, where the block of the school buildings is. Down in the pit a knot of men stand round a pool of red mud. A trolley rattles up a sloping ladder, tips at the top, and drops a feeble quantity of earth and stones behind that imperturbable portion of the crowd composed of knowledgeable initiates. The Viking bottom has not yet been uncovered. The infilling is eleventh-century, done by the Augustinian Priory. Will the hole turn out not to be the dock at all, but something later, to do with Stephen and Matilda? They will have to come back and get deeper next year. But there was an unexpected burial down there, one, in a stone lined cist, and maybe he had been cut to death with a blow in the mouth. A sacrifice to bring luck to the boats that were to use the dock? The lower sky is flat yellow behind the school. A chimneystack in the middle distance sends smoke across. We listen, a disciplined horde. Explanations ring true. Of the 120 dead in the burial of the chief, the men were of Scandinavian dimensions and the women were Saxons, wives and girlfriends, says the Professor. His wife is a Viking herself, with quite an accent. She seems impatient at some other pundits who wear silly caps and talk too much. Money is collected in boxes at gateways, by her daughter and other students wearing jeans with holes in their knees. 'Nice rockery', someone says, looking at what is, after all, just the vicar's rockery, which we are passing to get back through his gate. We wait for each other amongst the multitude filing down the paths, checking which of us has Eric in tow. If someone had slipped on the spoil heap that string would have been of no use at all. Heels were dug in and ankles began to ache. A smiling, talkative family helped us to some steps, offering their hands. Headlights in the road. The concourse breaks up in streams.

July 1987

In the late dusk the sky has emptied clean, then begun to fill with spreads of more continuous cloud, lit by the last sun. Jan and I walk out down King's Farm track, right to the Westleton road, then left, out towards the sea, and round by New Hangman's Wood. The air is motionless. No traffic. A distant dog. Broad, curved, full bracken heads don't quiver, and a million delicate birch leaves hang untouched. A hollow evening, with the sense of cool echo. Two robins chink, one hopping up twigs to see us, flirting his tail. Gnats bite along my jawbone, on my neck. Every now and then, in the bigger woods earlier, we heard a gathering hum, and found a lime tree with bees still bobbing round its flowers, high over us. Honeysuckle. Rawer sewage smells in patches. Small moths dip and wobble. Then a nightjar churr rattles in the middle distance, unmistakable, if muted. Our feet deafen us, but it continues, further off. Coming near to emerging from the trees into the gorse, we are halted as it opens up close by, hard and all-powerful. Stops. We step forward, and the bird itself tumbles, with a silent twist, across the sky ahead, in clear silhouette, hawk thin, pointed, long wings and tail, slender, with a series of single 'quick' owl-like notes, into the scrub. A toad moves sluggishly off the wet path. There were flies with black bodies and red thighs, and a round, ladybird-like beetle, packed into the empty calyx of a purple nettle.

Speak more about the woods. They are on the Mumberry Hills. The paths, however sandy in appearance, are flinty in composition, and they crunch. The ragwort is tall and stripped of leaves, with cinnabar caterpillars stuck about, high on the stalks, up to the flowers. The robin's chinking was stony. One car passed us, and stopped, unaccountably, in the middle of the track, some way behind, before pulling away again. We saw no one else. The darkest place was the lime avenue running down to Tin Houses corner, where we could not remember where to turn next. Whatever the Tin Houses were, they have been replaced by a new building of that kind of expensive, oily dark-red brick and black tiles. Pigeons smash on their take-offs. Hedge-woundwort stinks when crushed, a scent to go with its dark red, just as the cold, loose flaccidity goes with the black and gold of the cinnabar caterpillars, and the dry wiriness and fibrous strength as you tug and twist a bracken stem. It swings its weight against you, brushing you strongly, hefting so many rows of salivaless teeth. The black mulch under it, the brief slime on roots, the broken fungi, white in the grey-brown half light. Puddles, almost always with smooth, rounded margins, are deep in the ruts. Reflections of the trees shoot down into them, into a subdued, blue sky, and revolve slowly as you pass, turning in a world beneath. Brown and gold water, standing after last week's rain. The damp bit of squashy cotton thread, black, between your finger and thumb, fetched off your neck, was a biting gnat or mosquito. The damp cuffs of my sweater. The gurgle and splash of my full stomach as I walk, feeling high up, under my ribs. The ringing out of the tight, hard chipping of both robins, as they move around us, hidden, opening out the space, cancelling its leafiness, peppering glassy sound, so well known, yet here and now taking my memory there, more so than the nightjar's churr, which came so soon after… since that was more of an event to be told of and mentioned, rather than heard untold. It meant more than it was, while the robins were free of collection and could sound out without being appropriated. There was some triumph in the mineral tang of their calls, taps, urgently delivered on the here and now, their own warning of themselves, and us, so situated in the scrub, and nothing more. More than cool. Hot and cold. Not for harvest. Worry, yes, but of the instant, self-consuming sort, used up in the delivery. They bang off the board like annoyance, of the spontaneous, unmumbled sort, a cleanness of noise, unlooked for, registering. They prevent one dreaming of possession. They don't cause a leaf to shake, so the unshakenness is more and more because of the run of their rattle. Remarkable.

15 August 1988

Near Bourges, travelling south. The motel at Fussy, again, the same one we stayed at eight years ago, on the 15th August, 1980. The same row of rooms opening onto the courtyard. Richard's Peugeot parked there on the gravel in front of the rooms. Eric and Ruth next door one way, their voices coming through. Ailsa and Richard are talking on the other side. Spurts and rushes of showers spouting and toilets flushing. The double shutters over the door are almost closed, and only one of the lights over the bed is working, so the room is dim. I recognise features. A weird sense of recognition. Could one ever have expected to be here again? So much a place that you passed through that it challenges the memory to set out what, without any encouragement, it has retained. But here is detail. The pine ceiling is stained golden-brown. The wallpaper has green vertical stripes with golden motifs in them, and broader stripes of grey, with white curlicues as well as the green and gold motifs. The carpet and bedspread are green. There is an extra bed folded up against the wall, topped by a shelf and showing its springs. And a sideboard and a table. All the same, but used for another eight years. There is a black patch of damp, with peeling paper that has been pinned down. The paint is chipped and the shower looser on its swivels. Eric is experiencing pain from the fluctuating heat and pressure of the shower. But hair and body are clean again, hot with washing. This time we have had one night in a hotel further north. There is nobody here to let us in, because it is the Feast of the Assumption. The new proprietor, M. Gibarroux, phoned England to tell us he would leave the doors of 5, 6 and 7 unlocked, but we would have to feed ourselves. That is a welcome independence after the bar, the clients, the tight staircases and the tables on the pavement outside, of last night.

A long, long straight road down towards Bourges. You reached a crest and saw it all the way to the horizon ahead, with the great cathedral appearing momentarily, far away still, on the right. We will get there tomorrow. Today we called in at St. Benoit once more. Now Eric enters, blowing a cardboard nose flute quietly, to imitate an owl. He leaves the door open and the carpet turns mustard coloured, and all the greens in wallpaper and bedspread shine more yellow. A few hours ago, I am reminded, I was looking for the first time at Micrommata virescens, Bristowe's favourite spider. This one was female, a lovely clear lime green with sparse white fur, and black spines on her legs. Her black eyes were rimmed with a raised, grey circle. She had black hooks on the tips of her feet, which she stroked through her nut-red, curved fangs. Seen against the light, each leg had its glowing, green core with translucent yellow sheathing. The white mist on her abdomen, like that on a gooseberry, was caused by the white hairs. Her cardiac mark was a darker green dagger. Her cephalothorax was wider, short and broad. Barbara caught her running on her clothing as we were eating a picnic in long grass, in a ride in a wood. There was vervain, 'with heye stalkys, many smale brawnchys, small bloysh flouris out of hym lawnchys', springing and forking and peppering the place. And hardheads, with fritillaries tonguing them, and lifting and dropping their wings as an automatic action while they drank. Dragonflies patrolled, and bush crickets, green ones with black legs and long, elbowed whiskers, shook the grass stems.

The polled lime trees are there along the south wall of Fussy church, but there has been much removal and renovation between the church and the main road. The window, where I looked down into a lamplit hallway, where a hat hung on a hook, somehow so charged with someone else's life as we were passing by, and those tall walls either side of a narrow street, which I recall as making the village, for a few yards, into a little town, have gone. There is a car park, and a group of new shops facing the west front of the church, a charcuterie, even an Interflora, and there is a forecourt, enough for cars to turn on. We tried to look through the keyhole of the church door, as we did before when we saw the priest inside, alone, up at the altar, but now there are two keyholes, one blocked and the other black and empty. And the night is now tense and the air too warm. There must be a storm coming. A puff of sparks, high up, is a rocket exploding with a soft pop for the Virgin. The mill race is as loud as it was before under the rotten boards, and the smell of sewage there is the same. But beyond are open fields, a flat road, young trees in rows with strips of dead grass joining them, as if they had been set recently in a trench. A grey-haired man, balding, dressed in blue, and with only one arm, is walking a field away from us, accompanied by a cream coloured dog. He is going to meet a brown horse, which is advancing towards him, nodding its head emphatically as it comes, thrashing its tail and picking its feet up ostentatiously. He pats and strokes it, and it follows him, butting his back gently. No priest, but an old, one-armed man and a horse that is pleased to see him. No storm yet, either.

We go back to the motel and drink some brandy, sitting outside the doors of our rooms. More rockets go off. A cloud which is exactly the shape of a heart passes over quickly. It strikes me as an unusual shape for a cloud. I find myself dwelling on it and on the fact that this is the Feast of the Assumption, and also that we are here, against all sorts of odds, in Fussy for the second time. The net curtains are not moving. Then, inside, at the double, with the rain roaring on the roof, and the feeling of lifting off, rising upwards. Our suitcases are on top of the car, wrapped in black plastic sheeting. The rain slackens almost at once, so much so that it is almost inaudible. I step outside, where white clouds are replacing black ones. There are no lights in any windows, in the motel or in the adjacent houses. We are the only people here. The street lamp shines into the courtyard onto wet gravel. Concrete, which was protected by the overhang of the eaves, is smooth and warm under my bare feet, and the air has no chill to it as it touches my bare torso. Water trickles in the plastic drainpipe.

August 1988

At the corner of a street in Tournus, a fledgling pigeon, I suppose, big as your fist, yellow fur sparse over white flesh, muscular, spiky wings, closed eyes, rather hooked beak, big head—thuds to the gutter. It convulses, opening the beak, heaving itself over with the stubby wings. Silent howl. We stand shocked. A man continues to scratch the surface off a card to see if the number revealed shows he has won a prize. He looks at the bird, identifies it with one word, unintelligible to me, and goes about his business. To pick it up... touch it... writhing... strong... hurt... horrible. Take it... where? What would they think? No one else bothers to look. Damaged beyond help. City gutter. So glad as it goes still. The head lies over and legs stiffen in the air. The others go on shopping. I watch. It moves some more. Then it doesn't. I go to the Abbey, then walk round outside, see the Tower of the Doves, built by the abbot after the tenth-century sack by the Hungarians, so the plaque says. It is dried, egg-yolk yellow, like the fledgling's hair. I walk back through the streets and can't quite find the place. Then find I am at it. There he is, a few feet away, turned round but absolutely still. Leave him. To die where he fell. People stepping over him, cars within feet of him, dirt and refuse close to him. But he lived here. I go back to the Abbey, the streets seeming filthier, screws of paper towel with stains, blue plastic bags tied up, full of refuse. The Abbey tower is the dirty grey of many house fronts, but rimmed with brick red, a thin line of that down the dark grey tiles of the roof, the same colours, purposefully used, without stopping being the crude materials. Lombard strip work. The stones that make up the pillars inside are hard as solid glass. The big, cream blocks have been pitted deliberately with regular blows. They are playing the piped music again, the Hollywood choir this morning, and again the flute soars, floating with a sting in the hollowness. The columns are ten times as high as anyone walking under them. The arches are tight, narrow, not swinging. The place is opened upwards. Everything anyone does is emphasised in the height, the simplicity, the size, the rosy colour. Coming in from the narthex, through the unadorned round entrance arch, is really coming in. People do it in different ways. Folded arms, looking up. With a spring. Turning to prop themselves against the nearest pillar. Or heads down, thinking or reading. Instantly many are dominated by the word. They go round reading everything that can be read, screwing up their eyes, coming half way along a pew to see a plaque. An elderly man with his arms at his sides, head lifted a bit, eyes hooded. Then he helps his wife out from the pew, by her elbow, and on they go, not looking up until they reach the notices by the door, where they halt again. A young mother and a toddler... light blue boiler suit, royal blue sweater, walk hand in hand out across the reflecting floor of the narthex, against the fluorescent tubes above the display cases on the far side. Last thing of them is the reflection of the mother on the exit door, after she has passed through. Lavender sweaters. Green jackets. All set up by the rosy stone. I am caught by surprise by a young figure, leaning, arm bent, hand head-high, against the front left hand column in the north aisle, turning his face, wearing scarlet. For a second it is a robe, and there is a sense of ecclesiastical power. Young. High placed. But the red garment is a knee-length anorak. There are jeans below it. Yet, leaning against the bottom of that huge pillar, looking at ease, and young enough to be challenging, and bright scarlet... a touch of awe. Outlined against the brighter twelfth-century work.

To read the notices. Because they speak of the self, the familiar codifications, not of the other, as do the pillars and walls and vaults and apertures. These are body talk, not explanations of the sort the inscriptions articulate. Gesture. The open beak of the dying fledgling, wide and silent. The body screwed up at the moment of its being given up, or taken away. The head stretched up at that last active point. St Philibert's takes the opening and reaching and holds it permanently, and without the agony and self-reference, and pain. A calm, complete going. The gesture of the fledgling, and that of anything else like that, in here, contained and assimilated, lifted and opened and held. The opposite of the fall, unfledged, from the roof into the gutter. The snag of my broken fingernail, consolidated. The closeness and speed of the lizard's body, simultaneous, all over, gathered. Raised like a lake surface. The water surface matching the shoreline's intricacy in total detail, all round. The touches of diving terns on the surface. Slight. Or the touches of trowels, firmer. The separate slaps gather into one floating flute note, the abrasion and worry of the close flutter of the unexpected owl's wings, the bird springing out of what one thought was an unpierced, immobile wall, fitted, now, into the floating music, and most important because of that, the better that it comes as alien like that, and then is included, without losing the blow, the impact in the gutter. The image that comes unexpectedly, not illustrating a predetermined thought or mood. That poetry should be like that. To fetch out the sudden, shining fish in your bill. Riskily.

July 1989

Minsmere beach is shining. Beyond it the sea is low and an intense, leaden colour in the heat. Thin clouds scarcely interrupt the sun. There is a ladybird on every marram head. The damselflies drift and swing, electric blobs. Coppers and gatekeepers and a grayling on the path. White sand round bleached stems. Small, black ichneumons fuss and turn and jerk, searching, finding holes, disappearing into them then reappearing, seeming to have found nothing. Barbara, walking to the hides, sees a black and orange wasp straddling a green caterpillar, tugging it across the bare area towards the marram. She fetches me, but the wasp has gone. There is the caterpillar, however, and it is still flaccid. I go lower down, onto the beach, and here is Ammophila, longer than half your thumb, a pair of them squabbling in flight over a hole, making a disturbance which catches my attention. I fetch the caterpillar and put it near this hole. The wasps have gone. Ten minutes later one returns and finds the caterpillar. It steps astride it, curls its orange, black-tipped abdomen under it, and shoves. Nothing more. It leaves, and so do I.

An hour later I come back, after lunch, with Andy. The caterpillar is there, unmoved. After a minute, there is the wasp again, black and long, sweeping and twisting low over the grass. It lands, finds the caterpillar, approaches from the side and performs the same jab as the previous one did. But, instead of leaving, it briefly scours the area, ignoring the holes, and suddenly removes a compound lump of sand grains, which was obviously acting as a plug to a sealed burrow. It dives into the burrow, several times, to check it and to remove the odd grain. Then it fetches the caterpillar. Clearly it had only been testing before, or even giving a preliminary sting, because now it straddles the body and lifts it, jerking it clear of the sand, and moves at once with it across the few inches to the hole. It puts it down, enters the hole, reaches back out and pulls the caterpillar in. Seconds only pass, when, I suppose, it was laying eggs. Then it is out again and it begins to fill the hole. It scratches, like a dog, with its legs, spraying the sand backwards. Then it dashes inside for a moment, to pack and arrange the grains in there, and it does this several times. Each time there is a series of short bursts of sound, which I thought came from a far-off gull. But Andy correctly locates them, and they do, indeed, come from the hole each time the wasp vanishes. Maybe it is the vibration of its wings in the enclosed space. To fan the grains into place? But we can't see this, even when the hole is nearly full and most of the insect is outside as it does its tidying. But, during the last few times we hear it, the sound does open up, as if it were emerging. Nearly done, the wasp searches the area with brief spins of flight and much scuttling, for larger lumps, small pebbles, which it pushes into the neck of the hole, then fills round them with sand. The book says it might use a stone to hammer the surface down, but we don't see it do that, though it does include at least three such lumps in the filling. At last, after a more thorough examination of the environs, for a foot or more all round, it goes, and so do we.

4 August 1990

Better. Yes, better. Some of this is the genuine weariness, after travel, with a sort of firm loosening inside it, instead of the shaking that has been going on for a long time. We set off at 8 am this morning. Yesterday was the hottest day on record for England—99 degrees in Leicestershire. Substance seemed to be under attack. All plants were hurt, grass burned out brown, noises tinny and echoing as they might in a continental town in Italy or southern France. No movement was needed to make you sweat, and sweat was copious. I went to sleep here, in this same west bedroom, feeling I could drop a little distance and settle into letting things be, but the dropping seemed to go on a long time, a falling sensation in the diaphragm, with no arrival at a firm place. Perhaps now I am landed.

A pleasant drive here, curving off the main road before Stowmarket to visit Tostock, for the unicorn on its bench end. Off the glare. Drop down from 60 mph. Shadowy lanes again. Pantiles. Colour washed walls, cream and brown and green. The car is going well after I had it serviced three days ago, and an oil-leak quickly repaired yesterday. Here is the small, squared up, flint church. Time to open your eyes. The south door is open, and there is the noise of a carpet sweeper, one of those pushed by hand, back and forth on the nave mats. This is a sunny day, in another part of England, going about its business. Wonderful. A village, amongst many other villages. A most cheerful woman, grey-haired, meets us and tells us that the front three rows of benches are modern. So they are, but so well carved that they must be by the same man, I would guess, that Cautley encouraged in nearby Wetherden. The old benches and the new make a fine, solid set. Not as great as those at Dennington, maybe, because these poppy heads lack the full rhythmic invention, but here the animals are exceptional. Many of them have the dog's body and variations of the head, half human, but snouted, or flattened, or turned aside… often chopped off by a single, savage blow. The bodies are fat and broad, haunches right across the width of the arm. Round bellies. Toes like those of a greyhound. Wriggling pelts. A lion with a mane laid on in lozenge shaped tiles, and his tail quiff curled round his back leg. The unicorn, head turned and lowered so the tip of the horn rests right back down on its rump, consolidating the whole animal into a single and undamaged chunk. The 'famous one', she says. But there is a cockatrice on the other end of the same bench, with crest and wattles and only its beak chipped. And an athletic, long-limbed version of the seated dog, intact, muzzled like a Great Dane, or even a bear, but the body slender as a... well, as a what? A young mastiff? Again I can't come near to what these craftsmen thought. So many summers and villages. Were there sets of recognized animals, each different one with some point to make? Or was there free invention, and someone here who found himself comfortable doing the bodies of dogs? The young mastiff has his eyes rendered as little pyramids, as if they were shut, giving him a supercilious air. Did he smile his work to see?

Hammer beams. The roofs too are old and good, making it all complete and fitted overhead as well as down here. The woman finishes pushing her Ewbank... Yes! That is the name of the machine! Those wheels, with thin rubber tyres, and the revolving brush inside! Mother used to call hers that! A Ewbank made of polished wood. The clatter and creak it makes is distinctive, and I have had it in my head since we came up the path and heard it fifteen minutes ago. They suddenly drop what they have picked up in a little pile which has to be dealt with by special manoeuvres, or with a dustpan. She asks us to lock up and put the key through the letterbox of the nearest cottage down the road. Save her the trouble. Trust. We have left the car open, with luggage on the roof rack, beside the churchyard wall. Off we go again.

Hot. A pint of beer, gone so fast that the rest of the order isn't in. In the washroom there were grass-moths on the green painted wall, their upturned, feathery, beaked heads with the dead eye set back. Tiny monsters. Odder than the bench ends. Alien faces with unrecognisable expressions and minds beyond mind. A cream patch down the length of a folded wing, lavish in tiny loveliness. That would identify them. Colours suffuse as we pass on the side roads, under the afternoon blaze now. The corn, bloody in its shining depths as you glimpse in through the stalks. Whitened yellow, or sunburned brown heads, but blood coloured inside. Thistles are royal purple and covered with small humblebees. There is sparse shade in the lanes leading south towards Cretingham, where we look to picnic, briefly, under a single tree, just before rejoining more main roads, Dennington, the Saxtead windmill, the car humming along. Yoxford bookshop in its wooden shed. The woman here knows us, vaguely, as does Mr. Horner in the stores, not open until 2 pm. Well, you are not usually here until 4.30. His white eyebrows, slicked back white hair, hooked nose, anxious face. We fill a box with provisions, and go on to get the cottage key. That was a holly-blue, flipping across the pavement in front of Horner's. They are a feature of this year. 1990. The Year of the Holly-Blue. The carpet sweeper heard from outside the porch. 'You know what that is,' Barbara said, having gone in first and turned back to test me. She was thinking of Mother and her Ewbank. A sweeper, not an electric one, in a village church, in fields, with massive trees piled up in summer sun. A public house washroom, cool green paint, the feathered triangle of the grass-moth's head, the round, opaque ball of its eye, the stroke of cream down the wing from the shoulder, the cocked up nose. The fog of chaff round the combine harvesters. Dust in the air. Dusty moon. Falling. No bottom. A hollow stomach. Reflected light, in this bedroom, on the inside of the ceiling beam, away from the window, so that it is lighter than its shadow cast on the ceiling's plaster, or than its own bevel. But not so light as its underside, or the bevel on its other side, the one towards the window. And the shadows on the ceiling, for some reason, are doubled.

12 May 1991

I teach round the courses again, and reconsider as I go. For instance, it is easy to talk of Mannerism in terms of 'loss of nerve' after Classicism, about its adoption of multiple styles in a self-conscious way, its commentary on itself, its fracturing of gesture and state of mind so that they don't simply correlate, its observation of the body as an actor, set apart from a psyche with which the audience might seek to empathise. The status of the buildings as pieces with which one might not care to sympathise, but which are meant to be seen as a putting-together from here and there, a game that is played with counters which it re-defines as it alters rules. I shall be doing some of that again, doubtless, even if I don't think of it as loss of nerve.

What strikes me this morning, snatching an extra hour in bed to read, is how the Baroque is interested in relativity, as was Mannerism. In The Supper At Emmaus the points of view of the inn-keeper, the disciples, the chicken and Christ are different ways of understanding what is there, but shown without fracturing Caravaggio's style. It is like watching Mannerism taking place inside the characters, the watching itself being done in a consistently recorded world. Greenblatt tells me how when Sir Thomas More went home he felt that he had to talk with his wife, children and servants, and 'counted' this as 'business' which had to be done if he were to be more than a stranger there. He married his wife so that she should not be shamed, although he loved her younger sister. He 'framed his fancy' to her. Giulio Romano painted his frescoes of Constantine framed by Popes, done to one scale, Virtues to another, rendered as if they were statues, in niches or on pedestals, and between them the actual scenes, painted as if they were tapestries. So there was a multiple framing of the man who was himself converting to Christianity, with the heavens opening above, and new frames of reference descending to him. In the corner of the scene a dwarf apes a classical posture and tries on a heroic helmet, grinning at you, where you stand in the Vatican, grinning at you out of the painting of a tapestry. Mannerism, and framing. Even 'counting'. 'I count as business', said Sir Thomas. Life is bound to be framing and counting. The disciples at Emmaus will have to decide what to count. When you get to Tintern Abbey in 1798 and see, a few miles upstream, the smoke sent up 'in silence from amongst the trees', you will need to know how you frame that, how much it counts for, in your situation and in Wordsworth's. Does it count for enough to be worth an exclamation mark? Editions differ. The pool, in which the mother was said to have drowned her new-born child, was 'Three feet long and two feet wide', and how can you know what those dimensions count for, what they could have framed? And, in Prufrock what of the style where brackets intrude other ways of ordering things into the overall attempt to do so? And with Bernini, you were intended to look at the statue from one or two main points of view. But in Giovanni Bologna, earlier, you could circumnavigate the statue and all points of view were equally valid and invalid, one flowing into the next. Everything is 'in a sort' as Gonzalo said. It depends on how you sort it, which set you put it in. Meanwhile, it is only 'sort of.' And what of Chaucer's pilgrims?

Does it do you any good to let things roll? In this fortnight I shall teach a Wednesday evening group at home, of eight people, about Mannerist sculpture. I am rushing to fit in Eliot's minor poems in the last week before the sixth form leave. *Twelfth Night* is for 10B, and *Hamlet* is for the four pupils who are trying Oxford entry this year. They come together in the evening or at the weekend. I have reached Caravaggio in the General Studies sets. It is Lear for Lower Sixth Brown and Herbert for Lower Sixth Blue. There is *Far from the Madding Crowd*, where the valentine card moves from the frame of Bathsheba's mind to the solemn station against the mirror of self-awareness, on the clock that counts the business of time, on the mantelpiece in Boldwood's shadowy room, and, in Wallace Stevens, the blackbird has crossed from one of the many circles to another. Or, in 'The Kingfishers', the Mayan sacred bird has been seen with its feet and beak of gold by the Spaniards. Maybe I could do Pound, 'Near Perigord', to make it all explicit with the Lower Sixth after-school group. A 'broken bundle of mirrors'.

All of which is not what I use this journal for. But I shall forget what it is like, the flurry of it and the excitement of connections stretching beyond what you at first intended to mention. So much could be forgotten. But frame it now with Sunday morning, the lilac outside the glass, a deep purple, not yet broken open to lavender. I clipped the hedge yesterday, the twigs crunching and sliced between the wavy-edged blades of the shears, and I finished off by strapping a plank across the long, aluminium ladders, and hoisting them against the high arch of hedge over the gate, so I could climb up there and crop the wild sprouting at the head, fifteen feet up. Bursts of fragmented privet leaves, bits stuck to my scalp, in my hair, flying stems jumping from the blades, raw ends, the sliced skin of leaves, and the sparrows leaving in annoyance.

July 1991

On an early evening drive to Royer, to fetch milk. The cowsheds there are more hot and humid than I have found anywhere else. The sweet, thick smell of the cows is enclosed. There is a view along the passage behind their rumps, to a far door, deep, golden light through it, a man with an overhanging belly standing in profile. Swallows are diving inside, and through, and close around in the yard outside. A little, fat, dark, big-pawed, blunt-muzzled puppy is lapping milk from a bowl. One cow lies down. All the beasts are silent, seeming tired. There is a sickliness which is gratifying

56

in its strong evidence of a life-style, the density of it, the daily milking under the low wooden beams, in the furry darkness.

Sit on the bank, by the road, outside the pillared gate of the gîte. Grass blades, six inches long, soft enough to pack under my knees as my legs hang down over the low field, round which this deeper part of Dulphey stretches. Dusk runs to dark, and stars come out. Another windless evening. Sounds come sharp, local, yet audible everywhere in this cupped landscape. For a few moments, someone is hammering a metal rod into stony ground, the feeling of the materials entirely explicit in the sound. It does not go in well. Presumably he is repairing fencing for the rabbits, bred in the field behind. To my left, the Ebenisterie, long and lightless. Beyond that, the first puddle of light, outside the Cave, the Co-operative, where three children often play football at this hour, but not tonight. Then round to the right, to the first of two, white mercury lights, high, over the skip they use as a bottle bank, though that is hidden from here. And the old wash place, unroofed, flooded with stagnant water, thick with duckweed, except for the actual point where a stream pushes in and opens a crack of clear liquid. All hidden, far over the sunken meadow and to the left of the houses that cluster round that open space, with the well, and the pump with its long trough. The second, white lamp is to the right of these, in the space where the old, rawnpike tree grows on the raised island with the road round it, making a tiny square, closed in by houses, shuttered windows. The blank sides of houses whose balconies slant away from the square, turned aside, inward, or alongside the side roads. The balconies have steps leading up to them, supported by pillars and beams, and low walls, topped with rows of stone troughs full of red geraniums. The rooms behind these are usually inhabited, but those below, the old stables, are often not. One such balcony, with an outside, electric light filling it like a stage set, I can see. But there are no actors now. The last light, further still to the right, is in the farm across the rabbit field. Grasshoppers chirp from all directions. A car, coming fast, windows open, a radio programme blaring forth... speech... a woman's voice... not speaking but crying out repeatedly, as if in orgasm... from the Mancey road, down, anticlockwise round the circuit of this field, yellow headlights and quick, black engulfment following them, past me here and up the side of the gîte, back to the main road. Silence again. The voices of the others, playing solo on the patio behind the yew and the walnut. Clear words. Exact voices. The scrape of the plastic chairs on concrete. The hard and distinctive exists in the warm softness, as if its clarity were a chill, co-existing with a blur. A valley, all sides higher than I am, here, facing this field in the middle, with a track through the long grass across its centre, to the Co-operative. And another single tree, leafless, out there half way across, outlined against the lower sky which is pale, then, above that, a mild rose, edgeless, then darkening night-blue. No owls call, though one flew into the trees earlier, without a rustle. Richard coughs. In the villages, the tall stone walls, often rendered, and surrounding relatively closed spaces, make for amplified noise. Though the skip for the bottles stands free of the houses by fifty yards, the dropping of Richard's short, fat, green Belgian beer bottles down onto the wide surface of other bottles, which fill the bottom, many unbroken, is always traumatic, audible throughout the village. If they shatter, the noise fuses with the heat, and voices its force. If they don't, there is potential in the slightly springy, hollow crack. Maybe one should hurl them in, and set free a dammed back emotion, to hear it cut off, wiped out without repercussion, by the quiet and unstuttering, rolling wave of grasshopper chirps. So the mollification of the dusk in the valley has swallowed the disturbance of the car. The wiry, strong grass bank pushes under my legs, which hang down into the field, with feet to spare. With feet to spare. Think of the wicked slivers of white glass on the white, enamel sink, after shattering tumblers, which seem to give up and explode at a tap in the echoing kitchen. Think of the edge of the tin, opened with the poor tin opener, wrenched into twisted fangs, splinters of vicious, just bendable, metal. The tugging and turning of the cut out lid, to get it to come free. The solid weight of the metal skip itself, gong-like, though cracked and riveted, full of razoring pieces, white, brown, green, snagged with bits of flimsy paper and light, rattling bottle caps, snuggling blasts, herded weaponry, sharpened, wedged into a rectangular host, smitten into by heat, cooled, deflated, relaxed into chips, shards, opened up, loosened, rocking out until they fit, arms spread, in the silenced clank. In the uncontentious dusk, the scent of evening dinners eaten nearby, on balconies, uncontaminated food, the chippiness of bread crust, safely crunched, the dry shells of fragmented crust round pulpy white bread, in the basket, under the tea-towel which we tuck over it, to keep off the wasps.

11 August 1991

Evarcha arcuata looks violent and imposing in the tube, although I won't know who he is until I get home and look him up. I have not seen such thickened, powerful femora and tibia before. They are deep black, with the thinner parts of the legs brown with black articulations. He has a bronze head and a face-mask, ear to ear, as it were, which consists of two or three lines of white hairs, the top line pulled up to below his huge round anterior eyes. Above this the eyes themselves have white spectacles around them. And the beard, three straggly white tufts, hanging from the bottom lip, two of which are obviously white hairs on his chelicerae. It's a face mask that reminds me of the African ones on sale in that room off the courtyard of St. Philibert.

Three big, silvery tree trunks are lying, felled, in the corner of a field between Royer and Mancey. Grass, bramble and rose grow between them and over them. Their bark has not started to peel. And he was on them, black and active, dodging splendidly down into the undergrowth, obviously impossible to catch. He disappeared twice. Yet, somehow, he jumped directly into the tube as I held it towards him. The book suggests that their powers of vision give them scope to be curious, and that they stop to stare even while being pursued. So he probably re-emerged to take another look. He seemed to establish some inter-connection with me, in this ocean of random wood and field, the crop of sunflowers, the lumps of turned brown soil, spiked with chopped stubble, the vine fields, rattling jays, and the run of recent incidents which never much declared themselves to be significant. He can jump eight inches. When I release him he jumps well over a foot down off the side of the log.

This one of a hundred valleys is labelled 'sous la Rougie' on the close-scale map, and is under the eastern flank of the wooded range, La Montagne ou Vanniere, running south south-west to north north-east from Martailly les Brancion, past Royer, up to Mancey and then Ragny. It's the mountain we cross as we come over the Col des Chèvres most days. Thus located, we meet, Evarcha and I, I in my straw hat, he in his dance mask, interested in each other, and parting as equals, without, I trust, a cloud of distress left behind the hedge. In the bright fields, at a nameless corner of a path where

Richard could pull up and park, while we took a walk, briefly, in the cooling day, which is Sunday, 11th August, 1991. A few other cars pass, surprisingly, since the road is so narrow, only a white one on the map.

Weightless, multidirectional, seeming to float through the air as he jumps. Then stopping, sidling, sprinting, looking and finally plummeting into the grass for good. To be able to jump so far with such short legs. Full of tricks. A happy meeting.

August 1992

So long since I wrote. A year. Who cares? What then? Little. Not really any better. No change after the journeying. Four of my department ill and off. New syllabus not even published yet. And so on. Early morning waking most of the time, and violent annoyances.

8 pm. Lime blossom scent. Westhall church. Close the door. Your ears are switched off. Low sun coming through the west window reaches all along the nave north wall, gold, pinker on the rectangle of older plaster with the St Christopher, full of sheavings and separatings, pinchings and loosenings, silent stirrings of light. The chancel beyond is pale green, not penetrated, motionless. Also the Bohun aisle, bone-white, uncaught. Not a single fidget. Gold and green and bone. What it is, this evening, is this: glorious. Glories. Aureoles split and stretched and quivered, quivering. In a hush which lifts it beyond all normal uses, messages, instructions. The two white-haired women and elderly man here were wanting to know about horned Moses, about how a blind arcade could be blind with a window through it, about why there is panelling on the wall under the window by the pulpit. Delightful to find people engaged in such investigation, with a mind to it, placing and stating here, where, as they say, it seems so remote you feel you have found it. But the glory is not in these quibbling sorties, however innocent and however much a way of paying tribute to what is. The unspeakable standing of silence, stillness, insistent, gentle, combing gold, set in dead white and cooled-out lime green. And the sweet smell of lime scent outside, carried across the gate by the quiet wind. Astoundingly full, undiminished, attending to the changes of light through every day,

never losing connection with the whole world under the sky, but never less than complete, as it is now, and now, and always for hundreds of years. Like the grass heads, tall, seeded, between me and the dropping sun, as I go back across the fields by the dry brook. They sway, lissom, springy, and carry heads of all I've ever seen of God's fire. Bending banks of them along the edges of the corn or the stubble, curving up higher than the nettles. But, simultaneously, nowhere at all is so stark as just matter, as is uncommented Westhall. Dried. Shrunk back into itself. Juiceless. A genuine fright, as a touch long ago, and dry stone, the brown with no red in it, the powdery, the bat droppings in their collection, each on its shadow, all unmassaged, untickled by fingers, out there in unmoved air, and claiming your hands and feet as stuff, as they are themselves, as fine dirt. A skull in your head, knocked if tapped, under a certain covering of skin. The utter loneliness of all things in the extensions of time and space, left and left and altogether left, so that even the fragment of freestone you take with you in the glove compartment, on the dashboard ledge by the steering wheel, means that the journeyings of the car never take place, since all place is intraversible, still, in the speeding that can't be taking it away. The car stops in the stone. The stone stops in the car. And the grass stems bend so much, if you feel them, then snap. You know the exact dry feel of that snap. Flesh is as grass. Not merely in the analogy of gathered in and burned, simply as matter of touch, outstoodness, there in the pointless points, the weight of trouble, constant ending and left behind. Grass heads burn, lucent, constant, lovely, silvergold sprays of thin, ranged flecks of flame, like water halted, but are clusters of husks on hairy shafts, hair thin springing, which, when you touch, you have not touched, because their thinginess is so dense, so alien that, though it dents your fingertips, the dent takes the fingertips away from you, into the place beyond, and your knuckles and wrists, and the rounded bones in your elbows, in the meat of your arms, all at risk, half gone too... as the bent stem stiffens and snaps. The walk. Across four fields, along the choked stream, to St Andrews. The supernatural suggestion, gross as a real goblin, in the stationary bushes, the edgeless blandishment of summer night, the sudden click of the meter, or cluck of the fridge, the bony face of a little old man peering over a bench end, child height. But the stubble cracks under foot, hard in its snap, dusty in cloudy, warm scent. The late butterfly is whiter than normal, slighter, has settled, has green blurred veins under the wings, a green-veined white, and its paleness spreads, helped by the blue of a holly blue, also out late, flitting by, quickly done, into the empty paleness of the Bohun aisle, tall, whitewashed, dirty, cobwebbed, full of dead touches, yet here, still. Heartstopping littleness of the huge space. The unreasonable strength of everything which is nothing more. The Virgin's flask. The glass carafe. Precious free electricity, one coin to light every window ever. The rigid night.

August 1994

Westhall again. Overcast weather, unstressed. The Bohun aisle is where whatever is about to be could be again, but nothing is going to be taken by storm. The colours are comfortable, and a tractor is ploughing somewhere nearby, so silence and remoteness are only inferred. No thistledown comes in, even when I leave the door open and there is a draught. Here are the sixteen bench ends to the south of the aisle. I get to know their poppy-heads some more. Eventually I put my panama hat on the third one from the back. It punches the folded crown half out, and the hat tilts as if it were facing along the bench towards the head at the inner end, against the wall. As if it were pushed back off a forehead. Its straw is slightly brighter and more assertive than the colour of the walls, its black band a trifle darker than the wood and the shadows. It stands out. It makes the head into a head. I am aware of how all the other heads, fifteen of them, look straight to their front, but are only pretending not to notice it. They refuse to look. Even the one facing it does not focus on it, but stares rigidly through it. I begin to play to that. I walk away, up the aisle, and look back. From behind, the curled sides of the poppy-head emerge from beneath the brim, like long hair, swept up at its tips, left and right. A woman, wearing a man's hat, or a youth with long hair. The neck is very much neck, and the shoulders shoulders. As I circle round, and catch it sideways, the face is not there, only flatness, but again, from the north, from any angle behind it, a person is rather shockingly present, with something, too, of a scarecrow. The hat becomes stuff, because it is on a thing. The poppy-head becomes human because it has a hat on it. The exchange rocks to and fro interestingly, and a little worryingly. I walk up the aisle as if to pick the hat off. Then I don't do it, but step past and spin round, quickly. Yes. The other heads are pretending even more strenuously not to be surprised, not to be at all concerned, but the swirls of grooves on their faces are raised eyebrows now. But not one of them was tricked into turning a hair, or blinking. They are jealous because they have no hats. Yet wearing a hat is a pitiable thing, unworthy of a bench-end, and the third one up has been reduced in status as well as enhanced, humanised. Humanisation is not all benefit. It involves playing games. For this reason, too, the others don't look. They are embarrassed. One of them has been changed, probably for ever. Always it will be the one that wore the hat. I am tempted to move the hat to the head facing it from the inner end of the same bench, to even things out, since these two face each other, always. But that would spoil the variation I have caused, blunt the distinction. The inner one can remain the one I especially chose to leave unhatted, and its expression will always register that. It knows I have it at my beck and call like this. Its rigidity and changelessness say that I have decided, it knows, never to put a straw panama hat on its head… indeed I have decided to leave it, for many, many years, looking at its fellow, who did wear my hat. Will the hat-wearer be apologetic? Quietly satisfied? Twice more I walk past and don't reach for the hat, just to tighten up the implications. But the point has been made. I take the hat off. Now, in its identity with all the others, this poppy-head is forever different. I think it looks a warmer brown. But, I have to admit, when I look at its neighbour, two from the back, that is, if anything, browner. And, of course, my own head, when I try the hat on, is a bench end. Oh yes. It was strange to walk right away, up to the chancel screen, and turn back and see the hat far off, suggesting someone sitting with his back to me. Another person in the church, stiller than I had been. I placed my hand on the shoulder of the bench end, while it was still wearing the hat, in a friendly way. The hardness of the thin wood conveyed determination not to look a fool, not to give way at all. Its coolness was a little like shaking me off, refusing comradeship. Stop this foolery. Now I have the hat again, and benches can be benches. No. Not so. Never, I guess, again. The sun has flooded another poppy-head now, one in the benches parallel to the aisle, up by the altar. Choir benches. All the detail of this poppy-head are enhanced, its grooves darker, its grain clearer, the tip of its head and ears touched up. I speculate on putting the hat on it. It calls out for it. Instead I stand at the back of the aisle and toss the hat up over the rows of benches, towards the front. To see it fly. To hear it drop. To see it land on that illuminated poppy-head. It doesn't reach the front, but planes sideways to the right and flops down weakly, in a rather muffled, unreal way, not smacking down but sounding broken and inconsiderable. I go and stand by the sunlit bench end that it didn't reach, and, of course, it is the one with a knothole in its heart.

And now, years afterwards, the hat has worn out, with a hole where I repeatedly pinched its crown to take it off. The hat is finished with. Yet it is not. Here it is now. I can feel the peak of it between my thumb and the inside of my forefinger.

7 May 1995

Off to meet the Wheales and Barbara at Rothwell church. Sunday. On the car radio there is a fine programme about seventeenth-century music, John Bull, Henry Lawes, about the fantasia and the English reluctance to move on from the fantasia, a reluctance lasting right up to Purcell. The fantasia was thought of as a microcosm, each instrument in the consort of viols taking it in turns to be the main one, and the form broken free from the line of the song into interplays of fancy. Which form mirrors the universal harmony and is thus perfect, not to be abandoned. This kept me happy, even as I passed the 'Delays Possible' sign. I kept to the old road, the Lutterworth, Husband's Bosworth, Theddington route. Not much traffic, and very sunny. I stopped to fill up with petrol and bought a couple of cold cartons of lemon and lime drink.

At Rothwell there were many people busy about the church, but I found somewhere to park in the road up to its west front, under some trees. It is the fiftieth anniversary of VE Day. There are tables just inside the doors for tea and cakes and squash. Plenty of earnest ladies. A little girl, crying hard. The displays around inside the church are for the Land Army, the RAF, War Brides, Our Leader, Women Volunteers, the Army, and so on. The event is combined with the Flower Show, so pots of suitably coloured flowers mingle with photographs, helmets, bits of uniform, sheet music, and, overall, there is a warm scent. An elderly man is playing wartime tunes, carefully and not too perfectly, on a white piano. I go round twice and find myself including on my itinerary the charnel house, the bone crypt, which is also on display this afternoon. It is in a vaulted cellar, down a curved, narrow staircase, and has racks of skulls round the walls and a central, rectangular pile of bones, as high as my chin, filling most of the floor, so that you have to squeeze round it. A local man is lecturing. 'This one was a seventeen-year-old boy. Look at the sutures still open on this one. This is a female.' He picks the skulls off the shelves and holds them up in the electric light. The side windows have been bricked up after some vandals broke in and stole some specimens. 1,500 individuals are represented. Well then. Sentimental piano music and warm vegetation, photographs of Churchill and soup kitchens, French newspapers asking their readers to stamp on the swastika, a slightly hunched, sleek-haired man with grey shoes and pale trousers, looking, somehow, rather like a spiv, and watching me suspiciously, and myself, glimpsed in mirrors the choir use for tidying themselves up, myself with grey hair and beard, looking wry and uncertain. And over a thousand dead persons down below.

Time to go to the car park to see if the others have arrived. I sit there on the wall by the Market Hall, another building by the man who did the Triangular Lodge. What was his name? Then back, thoughtfully, to the front of the church, because these meetings are not quite straightforward when you are alone and can't check if the others are going to arrive. But there is Barbara on her crutches, and Nigel went into the crypt ten minutes ago, while Kate took Jack the dog for a stretch. We get ourselves together, sit on the grass, talk of poetry readings, then decide to go on somewhere else. Where? Twenty-four years ago I used to visit East Carlton, to see the Palmer monument. Why not again? We wind there through the lanes. The place used to be kept locked, and it is so still, but there is a notice telling us the churchwarden's address and Barbara saw the road that it specifies on our way in, so Nigel drives off and fetches the key, which, at first, does not turn in the lock, but does as soon as Nigel himself tries it. And here we are.

And here are the Palmers, life sized and stepping out of their urns, through the open black doors, looking up into the eternal light and listening to the last trump. They look as worried as they did years ago, holding hands, brown and dusty, hard to see against the window behind them, but, as you concentrate, they reveal themselves more and more as fine carving, just as I thought. Since I last saw them I have been to Chipping Campden to see the Noels, and Exton to see Lady Kinloss. I now know, what I did not before, that neither of these monuments, in my opinion, is as fine as this one. These Palmers are as good as it gets, except for the best works by Nicolas Stone himself. They are by someone later than Stone. Not, I think, by Edward Marshall, because I have seen his Lady Culpeper, supposedly his masterpiece, in Kent, and she is squared off and rigid and too early in style. By his son, Joshua then, who did the Noels, but is here in a more restrained, intense, less grandiose mood? The same concetto, anyway, of people leaving their graves. If not by him, then by someone without a name that I know.

The cutting is subtly facetted, not showy but never dull or simply smoothly rounded and soapy. It does a lot, but not too much. Her deep, narrow lips and wide-spaced eyes make her a Lely beauty, as Kate says. Silverfish have eaten away one pamphlet about them, but another translates the long, passionate inscription. His stoop is due to the shroud being tugged up to his head at the back. In this neat, dry, logical eighteenth-century church they survive from their earlier period, and he cares for her. We sit on the steps outside to talk some more, as we have so often talked. It is a quality meeting, for us and for the Palmers. Those cavaliers! Humour and conceit and the passions. The lady was exhausted in her forties by the 'barbarous age'. The doors are of black touch, hinged with iron, caught back on iron hooks. The conceit is that they are resurrected and coming out of the tomb. The Baroque development of the conceit in English tomb sculpture, which took place after Nicolas Stone. The churchwarden apologised to Nigel for the dirt on the monument. They had had estimates for cleaning it and were told it would be several thousand pounds. Should these statues be cleaned, anyway? Nigel suggests he has read somewhere that the sculptors counted on some deposition of dirt to enhance the modelling. A subtle idea! Would it not reverse the illumination, darkening the top surfaces and leaving the underneath ones lighter? You can see that these two figures were, of course, made separately. The join is at her wrist. Her hand was carved in his. The joint is now visible because they have been disturbed and twisted a little. But nevertheless, her distress and hope, his firmness and worry, her tremulous confidence and his solicitous sternness, they carry a weight of presence that makes real people of them. I believe he did only want to sleep with her in the urn. We drive off in different directions, to Shenstone, to Cambridge, as the sun lowers. When we get back, Eric is in the garden, together with clouds of gnats under the luxuriantly flowering lilac.
July 1995

It is not friendliness, even though each chair, each patch of sunlight, the wren's rattle, the shadows up beside the beams, the ten, very dry, darkened, stiff spikes of lavender in the bottle on the chest of drawers, are the same as twelve months ago. Ten spikes. They must be the same ones I broke and put there on the last morning, last year. It is a sense of time that has passed, and of importance. Yes. Both those things. And of quality of object, not just of importance invested by me. St Philibert is present in Westhall, and the Tempio is in Blythburgh. And in them are the furthest reaching consequences I can muster. And set against them, the absolutes of the sea, the only thing so big and plastic, and the shoreline, acute here as anywhere, and the sky, wider and brighter and most full of changing clouds, and the insect and birdlife... Once again the burnt out verges suddenly filled up when we were close to the coast, coming along the 1120. More cars... We were in a queue, behind the same caravan from Stowmarket right into the car park, now also a fairground for the day, in Southwold. But the verges suddenly had flowers with colours. A run of cream toadflax, the greater and lesser willowherb, hawkbits, mallow more than anything, as if its wateriness could resist drought. And beds of thistle with thick, greybrown down, which leapt up in wads and spread in the air behind the caravan, in the draught of its passing. As it went round curves it left the roadside tangle shaking. Bramble flowers, white touched with mauve and pink. At Tostock, in the belt of scrub and bigger trees, elm scrub, maple, maybe, where we again picnicked as we did several years ago, in a little clearing where large brambles shot up into the fork of an elm and then curved through and out and down, and held up flowers at their ends, in mid-air, face high... patches of sun around in the pleasant shade... several of the neat hover flies, Episyrphus balteatus, with translucent honey bodies marked with stripes... bodies from side view so thin and curved with hollow stomachs like inverted shallops, a beautiful hungriness, empty bellies, right for rapid flight. One of them rocketed off the flower vertically, then stopped, in a fixed station, in the air six inches above, solid body between blurring wings.

In Wash Lane, later, this is bramble again, arching out over the track, under the canopy that joins overhead, making it a tunnel... one that has not dried out in the heat, except for a rim of white and buff grasses, straggling in off the top of the field bank on the north side. Bramble and holly... Things hung out in space that is roofed over, suspended in the container. The banks have fallen in small cascades of whitish soil, leaving tree roots like brackets and handles. Under one of these, one curled, thumbnail sized, brown, desiccated leaf twindles, hung up on an invisible thread, in a current of air I cannot feel. Like the stranger in Coleridge's grate. Very small, but it catches my eye a second time as I return, having walked up to where the lane debouches onto the corner of the cornfield, past where the canopy opens, and bramble has made a wide, level bed, with green blackberries forming, still hard, amongst tonsures of brown hairs. Three or four small white butterflies here flap in a relaxed way, not entirely at random all the time, availing themselves of the space, but meeting now and then, winding their flights about each other briefly, or landing quite close together. They knit the place up, somewhat. And why this sharp and very tiny pain in my left forearm? A bug, half the size of an ant... no... smaller, and shiny, and with two white stubs where wings might have been expected... surely it could not pierce the skin? I watch it climb along the hairs on my arm, then it lowers its head and I see it has an extremely thin, but long beak, like that of an assassin bug. And this time I see and feel together, as it certainly drives it in. Was its abdomen so bulbed as Toricula elegantula's? The size, and general configuration would otherwise fit. Incongruous and significant, that smallness having that power, the minuteness of the hurt, coupled with its exactness. It lives on lichen on tree trunks. Emerald moss on the crumbling banks, a scumming over, elsewhere, of darker green algae, where the grains have not tumbled for some time. A red tailed bee, rigid on a leaf, all her legs flexed, a humped up stance, tall eyes with that not-quite-here texture of cellular surfaces, grey, a long front to her face, the forehead down to the jaws white furred. Sunshine as complex and complete on each wing, folded over her back, as in the whole scene. Ruth, through the branches, on the lawn, as I walk back for a meal. She is wiping the plastic table under the apple tree, in her grey and black speckled dress. See, as I stand on the lawn, the shadowy kitchen door, with figures, Julia, Barbara and Sue, and filled with a turning, churning, overlapped bulk of talk, one voice rising out and over another, before the former has done.

And later, out into the dark, by the hall door, put on that outside light, directly over the honeysuckle, which still has complete, wine and pink and cream flowers, and is diffusing scent. Static, illuminated leaves, into which tumbles a magpie moth, emphatically marked black and white, and gold and black on its worm-like body, amongst the glowing, light green leaves. It settles there and doesn't flutter. Some sort of small, grey carpet moth comes. Two or three footmen, signalling yellow in flight, then sober when landed. A custard coloured micro-moth, with red-brown, thin lines stained in v's on the top of its folded wings, and little dots of the same colour higher up. Its snout uptilted. Near the magpie and already motionless. An Agapeta of some kind.

August 1995

Sunlight gives skin cancer. If so Walberswick beach is a frightful place, blazing. This morning we are in a state of contention. So I run for it, alone to Westhall, where it takes an hour or two to wipe the mind, but it happens, it happens. The church is locked, but the middle cottage has its doors open, and a young woman sitting inside, and the key on a peg. I give it back to a smiling, bearded man, who whistles brief snatches of tune. Which I hear again at intervals all day... since I stay there till five o'clock. No one comes, and the cottage opposite is empty, though the front fence is newly creosoted, bubbling and smelling and shining. But, as I roll down the lane through the shadows, I pick up, at a distance, the scent of the lime, and I park with it trailing its twigs down to the car roof. A slight wind ruffles things, but I can hear the hum of flies and bees, and there they are outlined against the blue-white undersides of the leaves, inside the tents of hanging branches: humble-bees, hive bees and many, many flies. No bees searching in the grass yet though. Later in the afternoon I see one doing that. Once I have returned the key, and have the south door unbolted, I stand and watch the chickens over the fence. They have just been fed. There is a cabbage stump being pecked. They kick straw aside with violent, side stretched legs, looking up as they do so. As they peck, they bring their heads down in a series of jerks, not one, smooth, ducking motion. They peck at two, scrawny, brown young hens, who leap away with shrieks. They are Rhode Island reds, I decide, a few blacks, two big ones with scale-like feather effects—feathers edged with half-moons of black, round cream centres. One cockerel, who, later, crows with a tinny sound. At the moment they cluck and kick and jerk. There is a rectangular, metal tank by the gate, with rainwater a foot deep in the bottom of it—to do with the repair work I take it, since the tower is scaffolded, the wind occasionally hooting softly in a pipe. On the rim of the tank, a beetle, which I take to be Notiophilus, because of its racy shape, which I always think absolutely distinctive, and two, deeper punctuations on the elytra, which are otherwise punched with rows of smaller holes. And the bronze sheen—indeed so light and bright and metallic it is more like brass. But, as I peer at it, it opens wings and takes off, and Notiophilus is described as 'flightless'. Gnat lava in the sunlit depths, folding and twisting. As I reach the south door, to go in again, a peacock butterfly lands on the doorjamb, low down, and crowds itself into the crack, as if determined to get in itself, and knowing I am about to open it. So I step in smartly, and close it quickly. But, as I turn round and look up the Bohun aisle, there is a dark butterfly way up under the roof, midway along. Another peacock, I deduce; they don't move that fast. The aisle, I see, is a bright place. Always it must be, and maybe this is a major reason for my coming here. Today it is extremely beautiful. The sun shafts in at forty-five degrees, through the two south windows, stretching the diamond panes into elongated slantings down into the benches and onto the floor. Some panes are greenish, so the sun splashes on the wood are a mixture of lime green and rose. And the brick floor, although the bricks, unilluminated, are yellow-grey, is the same. The third bench from the back is like a long box of splendour. As time goes on, the shafts swing east, never crossing the aisle, so the five bench-ends with poppy heads, on the north side, stand with the gold puddle running across in front of their feet, until it has passed them by on its way to the altar. They look as if trying to be reticent about it, stretched and stiffened. Very cool coloured, a delicate dullness, but very orderly and steady. The butterfly keeps reappearing, floating and spiralling up in the roof. All bench ends seem attentive, as if rather dreading that it might come lower and settle on their ears. Eventually it does descend, and drops out of sight, up near the altar, without doing any more than flick near the eastern ones. I set a slatted chair by the tower arch, and sit there, up straight, like a custodian selling tickets to no one. Nothing moves except the sunlight, and that does it too slowly to see. And the black butterfly, cavorting high up now, and soundlessly. There is a swathe of bat droppings across the aisle, parallel to the front bench. Up above, the beam has a crevice along beneath it. The bats are hung up in there. Outside the sky is almost cloudless. On the tombstone of Joseph Balls a purple mite is laying an egg. I catch sight of its bright vermilion. Then I breathe on it and it goes crazy, rushing about hysterically down the side of the stone, and back. By half past four I am calm. When I touch the bench wood, however lightly, my thumb or fingertips stick slightly, and come away with a small kiss. The sun patches reach the choir stall poppyheads, the two facing west. They cross the left hand one and end, full, on the other, centred over the aisle benches, and with the knothole in its chest. It catches the sun shaft full on, all over, and nowhere else catches any of it, with the exception of one, small, dim patch much further west, on a bench back, easily forgotten. So, as last year, by five o' clock, the one, central person is totally gilded in the otherwise sunken place, gilded pinkly and greenly, with a glittering headscarf of web. It seems a suitable moment to do my leave taking.

27 December 1995

Sue is over from Leicester for the day. The three of us leave Ruth and Eric at home, and drive out to Hanbury and Fauld, with hot soup, good cheese and excellent bread for a winter picnic. Warm sun and heavy frost co-exist all day. The podge of trampled mud in gates is rocky hard and the white ice in a small depression looks like the bottom of a milk bottle. Hedges, down below us, fan out long shadows, which overlap with the same shapes in frost, so that the frost print is rotating a few feet behind, taking a short time to melt after the shadow has moved on. There is an overlap, not a match. A hare lopes across a turf amphitheatre on the opposite slope. Bits of stick protrude, cocking up off cropped grass, looking serpentine and attentive, and so much detail is amazing. Even in brightness bushes can seem bears. A pale thing on a stump has gone when we look again, so it was a bird, though probably not an owl. Derbyshire is not quite misty on the northern horizon. A tight hat of ice-cloud begins from a level brim in mid space, far above Burton power station, otherwise the sky is mostly open. No wind. We drink ginger wine in the 'Cock' and the glow in it matches that outside. The crucified Christ in the glass in the south aisle of Hanbury church looks thickly drawn, and glum. Golden but depressed. His blood looks congealed and frozen. Someone has given the statue of an Egerton, in armour, recumbent in the chancel, a bunch of red flowers, upright in his right fist. At the back of the church the new social facilities are open, lavatory available, everything serviced and nobody around to check, as if the nuns' organisational powers were here even after all that happened and St Werburgh's body was finally removed to Chester for safety from the Danes.

We park in the church car park, and come back to eat in the car under the hedge and trees, with our windows at once beginning to steam up. Sun shafts pierce the yews. There is a robin about, and a black and white cat, stalking a blackbird. The vicar's family are lighting fires in the house and doing things in their garage. On the ridge of the thatched roof of the old house, the fox still approaches the pheasant, both cleverly sculpted in straw. Over the field the pebbles at our feet are alabaster. The alabaster of Fauld has been famous since mediaeval tomb sculptors used it. Its white is close enough to that of today's frost to be an odd combination with it, very similar where a stone is freshly broken and sparkling and grainy, but slightly creamier where it has worn. Sheep against the slope of the lower fields, seen from the hill facing them, stand against their shadows, and so appear edged round in black, and their gleaming is outlined. The fierceness of the overall cold is not adulterated by the warm sun. The windless stillness and the open position under the cloudless sky refrigerate us. Crows which fly across seem particularly appropriate. Their voices speak from specific places, located in the firm air. Tree trunks are green and black but never brown. Though everything is so evident, there seems an awkwardness in adjusting to your contact with it, so that the single strand of the electric fence, switched off, knee height, I do not measure and place until it is caught between my legs. Stiles require your thoughtful approach, and some summoning of effort to lift the body over. Stones, when you go to pick them up, are stuck to the ground, locked in solid. Nothing adjusts gently. Dead leaves are glued on ridged tyre tracks. Magpies wobble long tails for their landings. Silver aircraft go straight across the sky, very concentrated on ruling white lines. The neo-classic, mourning lady in the Hollins bas-relief is too composed, and does not suit the prickliness and jumps and stiff surprises of the world outside. She is too balanced. The huge monkey-puzzle tree is neat and dark in its upper parts, but swings down enormous bare-armed, elongated lower branches, out of proportion in their length with the correctly dressed head of the tree above them. These are gestures of exhaustion and acceptance that are almost outrageous. The shout of the man in the valley, bringing fodder, is too close to you. What is definite can still be hard to identify.

Bright precision works as if it were confusion. Whatever was on the stump has flown away. It looked exactly like a bird so you were sure it was not one. Don Juan makes Castaneda stare at a shape in the dusk until he can see it as a spirit, and he fails when he recognises it as a rag or a piece of paper. Today is the variation then, when the stick turns out to have been an owl. Where was the ginger? In the beech leaves and the wine in the glass. Where was the blue? Tipping a chaffinch, or frosted on the slope. Another winter picnic, another year of being here. Where was the significance? Pinch after pinch and never a snuff.

February 1996

Now back from a walk along the estuary, the Angel Marshes, which were in a steady frenzy with waves, dull grey, brightening in the sun, in battalions, moving downstream. The reeds were craning away from the wind, whirled and corkscrewed in sudden, violent twists. The pools between them were frozen into cakes of cloudy, opaque ice. Redshank, looking black and white, were jumping out from all along the edge, with cries and squeaks, to fly, with no forward movement, into the wind, then swirl away sideways. I lost the lens-cap of my camera, somehow, completely muddled by the gale and the cold, thinking that I had put it in my pocket, or it had stuck inside the camera case. But it is nowhere to be found, and, certainly, there was no chance to stop and look, and, anyway, it would have been blown far away. Then to Southwold, coffee, and, driving back, I take a stretch of the road too fast, lose all control, and we twist, first into the opposite lane, on the compacted snow, then spin right round to the left and mount the verge into a drift and the hedge, where the car stalls. The only other car on the scene, following us, stops, and I see the driver agape. Completely unshaken, for some reason, I reverse out of the drift onto the road, facing back towards Southwold, nod to him as he mouths 'All right?' and drive back to the entrance to the girls' school, where we turn round. I get out, but can't see any scratches or dents, so we drive on, the car feeling normal, back to Westleton for tea, still oddly unmoved. So. So much that might have happened, had there been more traffic, had we damaged the car and been stranded there, so much possibility on either side of what happens, a blur of tits jumping off the hedge, brambles rearing at the windscreen as we tilt up the bank, disappearing lens-covers, which vanish like a conjuring trick even when you think you are having thoughts about them, all caught up in the moan of the wind, the shove of air against your body, the distress of reeds and gorse bushes bouncing up and down. As on the Heath this morning. Baker's Lane has head-high drifts, planed vertically off, allowing cars to pass. Their sides are wrinkled like skin. They have long, razor-sharp corners, or are laid forward and over, like old-fashioned mudguards. The gorse facing them, across the road, is plastered with blown snow into huge cauliflowers. We meet a man who cheerfully tells us that, last night, he had to abandon his Escort out towards Yoxford. Then he drove his Landrover into a ditch and it had to be dragged out by a tractor, after he had waited in it until daylight. He was now walking to look for the Escort. Somebody's story.

What might have happened did not. Goldwater did not become President. A meteorite has not yet blasted the Earth. It helps to narrow down the line to what did happen, and strip the swathings of possibles away. But I don't know what happened, in any final way, as I drove off the road. Even as it happened I was blaming Barbara, blaming the tape of Russian chant we had on the recorder, both such crass miswritings that they have nothing extra to tell, because I already know that sort of cheapness in myself. I could say 'Fate'. I could imagine, do imagine, dead people looking after me. I can see the completely unexciting chain of cause and effect, inevitable among the impossible might-have-beens. 'Engrossment in the particular has more to do with ignorance than knowledge'. I assume ignorance, with dread, and drive on.

17 February 1996

5.15 pm. Up White's Lane. A subdued and neatened scene. Twigs wiped clean and black, the young corn lime-green in the dusk, under an opal sky with grey and lavender cloud. The strange gardens, either side of this track, are stranger still. There is an overturned urn, and a metal trough on its side in one of the openings in the hedge. There is a white obelisk at the far end of an avenue. All this I have seen before, but, this time, in the small copse which is the last bit of garden before open fields... and I have to adjust my spectacles on my nose and stare to be sure... there are figurines, set on top of upright rods. Little dolls? In fact cycladic figurines? There are flat faces, angled shoulders, arms stiff to the sides, legs together. They are a foot high, and set up on staffs which are high as your face. On one pole there is a conglomeration of rounded lumps which I can't make out at all, looking like a heavy horse-dropping. Two sorts of figure, then, at once suggesting male and female, as do the two stones at the end of the double rows on Dartmoor, one triangular, one vertical. All these here are set with their backs to the public path, beyond a wire fence, and four six-foot, pyramidical cypress trees have been set beyond them, though two of these seem already dead. Further in, many more little people, some much smaller, which could be no more than roughly pinched-out clay figures. There are dozens amongst the trees of the copse, in rows and circles. Hard to see in the half-light. What sort of a fane is this? Not a Greek one. As always here, there is nobody-else about, nobody to ask, just silent fields, a partridge calling, a late jay, the quiet murmur of the main road from way off inland. These well-known fields, but these figurines! They break up the accountable. Whatever might appear next? What laws of probability apply further off over the fields, towards where the Old Hall stood? And yet there is no tension, just fluent acceptance, as if this were a continuation of the drive I have recently completed, to get here.

For instance, round the big roundabouts, the centrifugal swing of the car, the smooth acceleration measured by the white dashes slipping past, the weaving across lanes, re-curving into a new road which opens ahead, passing the heavy lorries, some of them hooded over their cabs for streamlining, some trailing flapping skirts behind their back wheels, all stroking long shadows up the flanks of the vehicles they overtake. One of Ruth's old tapes on the cassette player, Fats Domino, so that the white dashes become tracers, the bonnet lowers its head and surges forward, the road surface tilts and flows.

I turn left, over the fields towards the north, and accept, too, without a shock, a large animal standing motionless out over the open ground. It has just emerged from the undergrowth where the Old Hall was. A red deer. For a moment it was a huge dog. Black Shuck. But never, really. The legs are thin and straight. Now it turns away and, noiseless, gallops into the dim, far side of the field, with some humping and rocking of its hindquarters. Lost against the distant trees. Not startling, partly because I am already delighted with the white smash of dead umbellifer stems matted under the bank, and the yellow, wood-wormed logs fallen amongst it. There is a low, new growth of fresh and fleshy umbellifer leaves. Natural facts in their reality that I reach for, stooping, snapping a length of dry stem and pinching it as I walk on, its stiffness and crackle just what I knew it would be. But, after the journey, so far, so quickly and continuously, with that momentum, I am not entirely present as the person fingering it. I can't find out where else I am, other than here, stepping in soft boots along the path on the verge of the field, but there seems an on-running process somewhere, not quite keyed in to this evening. This log, which I roll over, this stem, grooved and pallid and snapping in its fibrous way, they are the imagery of processes with which I have not completely to do. I am moving on, even when I stop and try to come to rest. The speed of the car, the pressure of one lesson after another for years, sweeping onward, these cannot be quickly switched off. I tell myself where I am, but don't quite believe it. What were the plants that are now dead spikes over there? What are these familiar seed-heads? I can't get hold of a way of caring enough to stop my attention wandering and hurrying on to the next thing, looking for some manifestation strong enough to catch hold of me. The rigid deer does not stop this. It flows away like an imagination. I don't know these hairy bunches of keys, hung up in clots amongst the twigs. What is this tree? I perfunctorily pick up, from the blurred ground, first an obvious ivy leaf, then some shrivelled, rolled up fragments of the actual leaves, for which, even when they are in my hands, if these are my hands, I can't sort out a name. And that was me, crouching under the tree, fiddling in the grass and new growth? Here comes a man, ten yards out into the crop, aiming to avoid me. He has a dog. 'Good evening,' I offer, and he answers, not effusively.

Back on the green, I sit on the seat under the lime. The yellow floodlight, on the pole in front of Woolsea, comes on and off, shrinking into a match, or suddenly illuminating right down the row of cottages to the mouth of White's Lane. Woolsea is inhabited. In our old bedroom, where the martins used to throw their shadows across, I see a light go out and a head beyond the closing door, out on the landing. Then the man with the dog emerges from White's Lane and cuts across the grass, with a strange… with a long… with a branch over his shoulder, fuel for his fire. Six feet long, and over his shoulder, and he crosses to what was once Mrs Flatt's cottage. The gate clicks and he takes the wood round the side of the house. A man carrying wood, fetched, in the darkness, for his fire, seen in the lamp's yellow light, on the edge of its range. Another distinctive, but unstartling, figure in this film, and I am watching, still passing, without much of a grip to slow me down. The procession wheels by in my dreamless sleep, men with trees walking, lime-green fields under a nearly lavender night sky.

27 August 1996

9.30 pm. Back, here, another year, another fortnight starting in The Old Meeting House, Wenhaston. The others have gone to the beach. Everything the same. The whine of quietness, high pitched, yet with an undertow of constant softness below, filling the room. A muffle round the head, with just the scratch of this pen out there down through space. Standard lamps. Wall lights. Shadowy ceilings between the beams. All the detail again, scarcely moved. The dried rushes in a pot. The round wall-clock, which never goes, saying ten to one, and printing its shadow upwards, behind a beam, because of the table lamp under it. Room full. Chairs hold their arms ready and steady. A small table stands tip toe on pointed feet, which meet slim shadow feet stretching across the carpet to join them. Brown carpet. Flower-patterned chairs and curtains. Thick red curtains that divide the room, pulled back. The rag rug at the fireplace. Fire dogs attentive. So many objects multiplying so many shadows in the fields of the five light sources visible from this chair. All soft. All a comfort in the sweet, musty scent and the unending squeeze of the blood in the ears. Intact.

Great joy at arriving here this time. More than ever. To find it undamaged and very complex, at the end of the five-hour journey. Full and still.

The house back at Pinfold Hill set to rights, the whole accumulated system. Door closed. Roll down the drive. Then move, far, far and fast, sweeping along. The dashes on the road pouring away behind. First the worries about what was being left... where were the cats when we came out? And what of the electrics, the gas, the water? I exacerbated the tension by checking a tyre pressure and trying to inflate the tyre with a foot pump, which let more air out. Eric and I had to drive into Lichfield and find a garage with a pump that worked. Was this a sign? Circumstances seemed liable, for a moment, to multiply difficulties and frustrate resolutions. Then the journey swallowed that scenario as if it had not happened, as if Pinfold Hill were altogether gone.

Hours later we were eating our sandwiches in Suffolk, beside the churchyard at Tostock. There was a butterfly, a painted lady, amongst the tombstones. Straw coloured, thin grass stems higher than the headstones. The church door was not locked, it opened quietly at the first try. Here were the bench ends again. Did I know that the unicorn's horn was grooved with a spiral? Had I seen his fine, sharp cleft hooves? Many a this and that. The coy, lowered eyelids of what might be a great hound. An ape with half his face chopped off. Some four toed feet, some three. Was this another unicorn, now headless, but with what might be the tip of his horn low down on his flank? Yes, if he had lowered his head as did the first one. But if so this one had the hooves of a carthorse. The squirrel had a thin rope of a tail. Now the pleasure of turning onto the 1120. The many separate white clouds in streets, to journey under. The orange incandescence deep in the stems of corn, necklaces of pink lesser-bindweed along its edges, or thin fringes of pale, taller oats. The orange cut up into blocks as bales and built into ricks. Park here, on the grass, round the front of the house, with the bonnet in the shade of the holly hedge. And step inside this unexpectedly generous sameness, perfect to an astonishment, a gratitude. The house here becomes, in a moment, something to count on.

A quick round outside to begin with. At once, on the end wall which has only the small window in it, on the dark side against the hedge, this big, grey froghopper, rather fat and kite shaped, like Issus but with finer dark dashes, more complicated veinings and with glamorous curved and recurved rims to his eyes and splendid, fitted neck-plates… not in the book. A male spider with long, annulated legs and extended palps with hooked thumbs on top of them… is this Meta merianae? The cephalothorax is right, the black head, the paracymbium on the male palp 'is visible with a lens'. Well, maybe. Very visible. Damp, shaded sites. Wash Lane is behind the hedge here, filled with dead umbellifers, brown, delicate, quick to snap, growing right out into the track as if nobody had been here, any more than, it seemed, they had been in the house. Butterflies on the nettles and bramble flowers at the field edge, as usual. A red admiral, soaking up the sun. Four ringlets, both rusty and ashen. The ice-blue, glinting pair of posterior median eyes, oval, cold, with the rest of her packed in her cell under a brick… Drassodes. This is a bagworm case stuck to the rendering of the back wall at head height. This is a pill woodlouse, Armadillidium, not a millipede, Glomeris, with the many small plates at its rear end, unrolling on my palm. There is the brown dragonfly hunting along the hawthorn. It's chilly now. No swifts, only a few gulls, crying for a moment. But it's all a collection, an array, a lot. And the book which Jeremy gives me for this trip, is, as I unwrap it, a collection of poems by Basho and commentaries on them. Basho and his Interpreters by Makoto Ueda. I open it to the one about shepherd's purse. 'Looking closely, I see… under the hedge'. The delight of the inconspicuous, the exact. To slow you down and wipe your eye. Reserves of the unspoiled. The plant is 'content with itself', one of the commentators says. Somehow I was not expecting so much, because, after all, you can't count on your own state of mind.

And there is the three quarter moon burning all clear against black, like a worn ball of pumice, pecked with white dots on charcoal blots, fully defined in silence, as last year, with a clear planet, Jupiter again, not far to its left. Seen in the scent of honeysuckle, which, now it is dark, is suddenly suffusing the area round the front door. Now here is scent and silence and clarity in the most enormous space. Clara has brought a huge sheaf of massive lilies, yellow, open-throated, pale mouthed, lightly veined green inside, many hard and heavy heads still closed, to fill two pots, one in the kitchen, one on the dining table, of a size to take charge in the multiplicity inside both rooms. How many beams, how many joints, how many slats, necks, waists, legs, tenons, braces, sockettings? How many finished tasks and how many things well done? How much for the lights to run shadows round and past and through? How much come together inside the rest? Enough to say this is best, here and here and here, like this.

After the rocking of the car on the uneven surface of the slow lane, making it feel as if it were floating, there was a burst of white pigeons somewhere, chips of snow over some village, over some rooftops. The car, heavy laden, packed tight in the boot, on the roof-rack, between the seats, as it weaves and shoots, passes and proceeds, swings right and waits while you open the gate with a scrape in its long, curved rut and prop it open with a stone. The white, rendered walls. Hot in the late afternoon. The pipes and cables on them, with webs behind them. The cracked paint on the sills. The stiff snapping of dry parsley stems, coddled in the wobbling dapple in the overhung track. The flecked and folded cape of the grey froghopper with his barbarian helmet, styled for goggles, neck piece solid, articulated like plate armour, who moves, worried by my closeness and stare, a few tentative shiftings of his hair thin legs, readjusting, thinking it out without a change of face. Hello to Blythburgh church as we pass and re-pass on our last few miles to fetch the keys. Even from the main road you can see through the clerestory windows as they angle opposite each other in a match, a row of instant, tiny bright oblongs, measuring your terms of space and speed. The flag is up on the staff. If we stopped to look closely we would see it replenished with bold rippling. But we must make time, be ready to greet someone, to fetch someone else from the station. Here they arrive, the car straddling the grass spine of the sandy track, as I step out of the dark entrance to Wash Lane and take off my new panama hat.

July 1997

Westhall. The sun is coming from the south east, filling the splays of the two Bohun south windows with slanting prints of the mullions and the tracery and the glazing leads, stretched top left to bottom right. Nothing of this spills past the rims of the splays onto the inner wall, or off into the aisle, onto benches or floor or onto the arcade. A considerable wind is tossing the horse-chestnuts and the beech, which send in these half melted notices of themselves, so that the shadows must be moving up and down in great sweeps on the outside of the wall, and so, in here, rush through the gridprints on the splays with a thrilling boldness and copiousness, pouring up through them, as if there were miles of available dappling below, up out of which they could be sucked and fountained up and away, out of the top of the framed presentation. The sense of an inexhaustible resource of excited, various availability, pulled up in an unstoppable inhalation, swelling the ribcage, ready for the contentment of an enormous sigh of acceptance, and then that dazed, swimming feeling that comes after that sort of sigh... the spontaneous, unexpected curve over and rest of delight in what has happened. So, here, the upstream wavers and turns and shatters into a silent, bouncing tumble back down, diagonally again, once more with reservoirs of infinitely varied possibilities above, that can spill or not, thin, or slow and stop, breathed out, relaxing. While this varying rise and fall, all contained inside the golden splay and ledge, all noiseless of course, is happening, there is also, within these shadows, a tightening and loosening of focus, as the branches outside move nearer or further away from the wall and the window. So, in here, the passing shadows can suddenly thin out, like ripples on water that smooth into the clarity of the reflection of nothing but an empty, yellow sky. Now, in one place, the shadow is emphatic, hard edged, then it is suddenly furry, molten, then vanished into plain, sunlit whitewash, even while the tumbling down, the breathing in, the dropping or swelling is still going on. So the surface and the depth co-exist, the across against the near and far, taking place on the one surface in a complex eventfulness, all seen and nothing heard. All sorts of possible comings and goings, approachings, recessions and journeyings, high and low, simultaneously. The whole river, and the particularities of which it is made up, little births and deaths in passage, a terrific wallowing, yawing, crumbling cascade, is registered, tuned in, tuned out, here and here and here. And look at the massive Bohun east window. There, too, the sun lights the splays, but no trees outside intervene.

The slanting sheaves of mullions and leadings are precise and strict and still. And the nave windows, under the arcade over there, further off, they have dimmed splays, untouched, cold and blenched, as is the rest of the interior, except for this hot business in the Bohun aisle. Only, outside, over there through the nave windows, the golden behaviour which is near me here, is matched by other trees, north of the church, seen straight through the glass, in their proper colours, cypress of cypress, lime of lime, just touched down a little and hushed by the thick glass, but continuously moving.

There is a wren in here again. He flies as if he felt his weight on his short, curved wings. He forces himself up into the roof, and sits on pegs up there, illuminated by the reflected light. He bobs on embattled transoms, hopping along castle walls. He picks up spiders. Against the nave west window he enacts an episode with a butterfly, buzzing at it, missing, the vibration of his wings against the twist and flicker of the other. He gleams up in the dark, or becomes a tiny, black silhouetted shape. He passes close to my head and I hear his feathers. There is broken glass in the east window.

November 1997

The funeral is over by mid-day. Eight people in the small chapel at Golders Green Crematorium. The coffin, mahogany colour, brass handles, rolled away into a further room. No furnace. One imagines people in there, sitting reading newspapers, waiting for its entrance. The chapel walls are clean brick. Three carers from the home. We pull ourselves through selected verses of 'The Lord is my Shepherd'. The clergyman gives a neat summary of what we told him, over the phone. Pauline narrows into someone whose interests are hard to enumerate; who had travelled, New Zealand, Australia, America, but who never much registered it. Silver hair. Pursed lips. White skin. Mopping her mouth with a handkerchief. New Zealand accent. Unexpected and rather funny denunciations of selected people. Mysterious past on the other side of the world. What happened to all her possessions, apart from these few glass brooches, one string of cultivated pearls, a bone shoehorn? These photographs go back no further than parties at the community centre in Kentish Town.

The yellow leaves on the plane trees, outside the windows of her room. Windows which tilt open in a framework, on hinges at the top, so that the gap is below them, a caged opening, the air, somehow, not coming up easily through their down-tilted mouths. The back street outside. But many yellow leaves and some blue sky. The bed tugged open. A screw of bedclothes, just as it was left when she got out of it in the night with a pain in her chest. Go through the drawers. Leave the TV to the home. Take this suitcase with these letters, photos, two or three boxes of costume jewels. This is all? She managed herself down to this. She left the bank as executor... to save trouble. We go on to its branch in Kentish Town, but the girl on duty can't find the will.

More yellow plane tree leaves through barred windows, with sun pouring in. Larger, unstuffy, shining white rooms, just hours after the funeral. Gordon Square. The Percival David Institute. Glass cases set out with porcelain. First downstairs. The orange rim, orange brocade on white, iron-red enamel, glowing, clean, unbroken. With four medallions, each containing a Chinese character: wan, shou, wu, jiang. Top, right, bottom, left. Round the flat rim. Ten thousand years of long life without end. Then, best, upstairs. The clouds of yellow leaves. Barbara resting on a chair, in the corner, by the window. The Ding ware, Song, Northern Song. Warm ivory tone, fired in plenty of oxygen. Fire and air. Fresh cream. Copper-bound rims with no joins in them, cut from one sheet, a thin, glinting mouth-rim. Eleventh and twelfth century. The objects that stunned the visitors to the 1935 exhibition. Some from the Imperial Collection, the Forbidden City. Collateral to the Yuin Yeh Bank from the Dowager Empress, departing in 1901. 'Lovely weather in Peking' was the message to show that the deal was going through. Bribed guards. Japanese dealers. The incised decoration is shallow, swift, or the moulded is more packed, but still fine, not breaking up the one cloud of light. Unshadowed. The bowl. Number 108. 18 cm diameter. Phoenixes, peonies, which stunned the Emperor Quianlung. 'Amid accumulated pollen and massed flowers the two phoenixes droop their wings.' His poem on the base of this piece. The copper mouth-rim. Round. Round. Round. Round. Untrammelled. Pure, warm ivory. Lovely weather in Gordon Square. Lemon burning plane tree leaves. Unglazed blue sky. Easy walking for ten thousand years on the pavements, the train not due until half five. Then a Black Ding Ware bowl with copper rim. The astonishment runs on. Into celadon, into Ru ware bowls and brush washers, quiet green-blue, the colour of ashes after burning. Air and fire. Gold lipped. Peace and calm, rounded and smoothed and circled and stilled and floating as sheer appearance. Somewhere is Pauline, sitting in a royal-blue dress with her hands folded in her lap, at a party, looking straight at the camera, eyes quite wide, mouth still pursed, just about to make a dry joke about being dead, about London going on through October into November, about Songware and the move south from Kaifeng in 1127, about green tea in celadon bowls and white foam, whisked, in black bowls. Highest quality. Guan celadon. Golden brown crackle deriving from within the iron in the body. The sparse cackle derived from the closed mouth and revealing the iron in her mind. The folded hands for the photograph. The elegance in the stuffy room, cheap pictures, trinkets, walking-stick hooked over the back of the brown leather, scrappy chair. Life is sweet. Pat told her that on that Saturday when she seemed worried her mind might go. Mindless Guan celadon. Thoughtless purity. Ch'an Buddhism coming into the Song synthesis. Taoism, Confucianism. 1175, Chu Hsi against the Lu brothers at Goose Lake Mountain. 'The work of easy simplicity, great forever and abiding, while, piecemeal, the affairs float and sink.' The younger brother, Hsiang-shan, has written this and reads it out, to confound the eclectic. No books. Folded hands, straight stare into the air, at the camera. The rest is footnotes, the sliced slippers and swollen ankles, propped on a footrest. Henan black ware. Oil spot glaze, like droplets of oil floating on water. Like eyes in a photograph floating on the occasion of the party she was asked to as one of the residents. White face. Dark slip. Few visitors this afternoon in Gordon Square, where, I dare swear, Pauline never came. Golden brown crackle in quiet celadon. Good luck Pauline.

8 August 1998

On the last day here I choose not to do much. I stand about in the long, low-beamed, downstairs room, enjoying the dimness pierced by the sun which comes in from the sides, catching on the many slatted backs of the chairs, the polished table top, always in the shadow, and the scent of the place. There is the cream armchair, its padding lax, beaten down by so much sitting, its seat cushions driven in so hard it is quite difficult to pull them up to see if any small objects have been lost down the edges. The side table is to its left, under the window. On that we put the most useful reference books, and the glass of water, which contains the plants still needing identification, reviving, smartening up, or lolling in resignation. The hairy brown carpet, that shows every bit dropped on it, crumb or fluff or seed which has wafted there through the open door, or leaf fragment brought in on the shoe from the grass immediately outside. And the bits bed in, so the Hoover doesn't pick them up first time, second time, third time, so you have to scratch at them with a fingernail to loosen them, or try to rough them up with your toe. The rag rugs, on which the Hoover chokes and bangs. The pamment floor in the hall, where it clatters, and the two loose mats there, carpet pieces, dark red and blue, loose so they woof up as the Hoover crosses their edges. The individual press and click as you switch on the lamps at the wall plugs, or fumble up underneath their shades to find the switches there. The green, plastic plate rack we bought years ago, on the draining board, its slots shallow, so the plates set in it tilt weightily, only just held up, sloping forwards or back, with the wedge and pinch on their bottom edges just about nipping them, a tentative engagement. Once a bowl did fall, but didn't break. The black plastic bag in the waste bin, the lifting lid of which Jeremy mended with a metal pin two years ago, fills surprisingly quickly. I tug it up and out of the bin, against the suction, thong its wrung neck with the orange plastic ribbon attached for the purpose, and shove it deep into the dustbin by the gate, against its hissing and puffing and blowing. On Tuesdays I carry the sacks, in the evening, across to the gate of the allotments, and pile them with others that appear there from the house up the track. This year there are not only plastic bags hanging off sticks over the vegetables, but a scarecrow made of some sort of shirt, with arms certainly, and a little bucket or box, upside down as its head, a head which, surely by chance, has slumped, so that it catches, shockingly, the attitude of a man leaning on one arm on the top of the chicken-wire fence out there, and looking down at his crops, meditatively.

Enough of this. The place has accumulated routines, touches on objects, their manipulation, sequences of movements done repeatedly with resultant noises, collisions, clunks, knacks. They are so specific when you remember them that the world seems impossibly full, a miracle of containment. Or does it leak? I take one of these biscuit-brown mugs, with a darker, redder brown design on it, and hang it on a hook, one of the row along the top shelf of the kitchen dresser. The thickness of its handle is a fraction too much for the curvature of the hook to accommodate it loosely, and the hook is plastic covered, so thinly,

I seem to feel, that it is almost hard metal but has a skin with a slight stickiness over it. So the handle of the mug jams and the mug does not dangle loose, it juts out. I push it back so that it is suspended vertically. That resistance to the easy dangle. The refusal to do it. If it happened anywhere else I would be back here in the kitchen of the Old Meeting House, Wenhaston, behind the table, to the right of the array of electric meters on the wall, to the left of the bread-bin, which is so full the lid won't shut down on the top loaf. Oh I wish that it were not that I will never do this again! If it disappeared, there would be nothing to mourn. If I had never noticed it, there would be nothing there. If I kept it, vivid and complete, it would be treasure. But it is leaving, skimming off into an infinite drop, as fast as light. The sound, I think it was a double sound, with metal and plastic and crock in it, and the sweep of my hand and wrist as I moved, in the business of drying the mug, stepping over, reaching up and hooking it on. The others in the room behind, their talk, the splashing in the bowl. The momentary jamming at an angle, the loosening and the arrangement of the final tilt. The mug is on the peg. I will never take it off again. Sovran melancholy. Herein lies the cause of the always attendant sense of my uselessness.

In Wash Lane, Barbara and Ruth having gone to Minsmere beach for a last swim, I part two cool ivy leaves. Standing on the lower one is a pale fly, one of those that are emptied of colour and, somehow, left naked, untinted. Clear wings folded across each other, front legs crooked up above the edge of the leaf, sunlight coming from behind, glowing minutely here, making his front knees rosy. His head is raised, looking away into the light, a knob of black hair on his forehead, shaped like a little square black flag driven in between his blank, carnelian coloured eyes, which catch the light like silky pebbles. He is not disturbed. He never moved the chair, and yet here he is, looking as if he were welcomed by the blue mountain. Further up the lane, under a holly, two wide open parasol mushrooms, the biggest a foot across, neatly scaled dark brown on cap and stem. Plenitude. And, in the east bank, a narrow hole with a short tumble of fresh sand below it, and wasps coming in and out urgently, so there are eight or nine, at most times, in the mouth, coming or going. What are they bringing in? On a closer look those going in have nothing, but those coming out have round pellets in their jaws, big as their heads. One walks a short distance on the approach to the hole, before she takes off, so I catch her in the plastic tube which I carry in my pocket to meet such contingencies.

She threshes about, still biting the pellet, until I tap the tube. Then she looses it and I let her go. The pellet is a ball of earth granules, fresh and tacky and packed together, with nothing inside it, as I check by poking it apart with a grass stem. Are they digging their nest hole? Carrying the throw-out a very long way before depositing it? They lift off, often staggered with the weight, making for the patch of open sky through the scrub on the opposite bank, then out over the ploughed field. They will still be doing it in half an hour, when we will have gone.

July 2000

We eat at a table outside Le Petit Rolin Crêperie, directly below the porch of Autun Cathedral, the Giselbertus Christ in Majesty overlooking us. A pancake with ham and cheese, loaded with an egg, which explodes and moistens the rest. The Fountain of Lazarus droops several thin spouts of water around the central jet, which it fires upwards. The carved pelican on top vigorously feeds her brood. Beyond that, the nineteen lime trees make their shady copse in the car park. The cathedral is pale grey stone, rather metropolitan, with the later, gothic, north flank cleaned and yellow, and the roof astonishingly tiled with mustard, sienna, orange and cream tiles, in patterns, glazed to a mirror shine. The porch itself is tall and cool. Blue stone slabs the steps up into it. And the tympanum. The mandorla. The face that doesn't look at you, and the spread hands, palms outwards.

A party of fifteen swifts harry the square, shrieking. They swerve into the porch and sweep up to the roof, right up to its ceiling, behind a rib in the vault there. Hidden by the rib, from where we are sitting, there is a round hole in the smooth ceiling, dead central, in front of Christ's gaze. The birds seem particularly big and very black, except for their flashing white chins. They approach the hole, flapping hard, then fall away without contact, usually. If two close in simultaneously, they tumble back, squabbling. But sometimes they partly enter the hole, then drop out again immediately, and, I suspect, because I saw one shoot down well after there was any fluttering visible up there—yes—here is another doing it—occasionally one goes inside and stays there for a moment, out of sight. They have to flap hard, then fold up to shoot in. Flap hard then pop in. Most of their approaches don't touch, a few do, but so briefly no feeding of young is going on. The hole appears empty with no little heads in there. Nevertheless some do go all the way in.

So, under the cool, stained, yolky cream and brown plaster, the sharp, black birds cut and flicker and tumble, noisier than the traffic, and nobody looks at them. Christ doesn't blink. The spindle-shanked devils mouth on, the souls are weighed, angels take the weight of the mandorla, Lazarus, Martha and Mary, on the trumeau, never glance up. A serious young man examines his diagram of the tympanum. A copper-haired woman takes photographs of it. The cave is echoing with thrilled shrieks and pulsates with obsessed energy.

The swifts are so fast and pointed and definite in their blackness, until they falter and fall away in awe of the small hole. They all are involved with it, want to come to it, but only the few dare. It is most powerful when, unpredicted, one snaps out and away, out of the porch into the city, white chin blinking if it comes towards you.

The swifts heft up, vibrate, wobble and sweep off. There is an occasional soft rustle, and now I hear it suddenly, and I realise it is happening exactly when, at last, one enters the shaft. There it was. I saw it disappear, and I heard that!

Do we read their blackness and screaming as devilish cunning? Or set no store by them at all, not notice them at all, ignore them as the pale, straight-faced Christ in Majesty seems to do? I feel like handing Him my binoculars. The spectacle this morning is the momentous hieratic scheme of reward and punishment, weighing and assigning, and Christ, hands held out, palms upwards, not looking, but, the motionless master conjuror, presenting the brilliant juggling of a troupe of fierce, fast, screaming acrobats. He has long seen it all and now grants it a showing without having to look. He hears not the swifts, but the four curved horns blown far off in the corners. He comes to the unmediated 'This' and 'Thus', and has thrown out both hands.

There is bird shit on the blue stone floor, the echo of sandals slapping. Outside here are yellow sunshades over the tables and our voices are stuffed into the thick texture of now, the hot air, the gruffness of a laugh, the tabletop warm to the touch. In there, the swifts sprint at their target, twirl in a cloud, make it happen, rarely, with one little rustle. Then they return and lace what has been done, and could, to what we are making of it, and to the ham and cheese and the hot fried egg.

14 May 2002

Sometimes you coincide with yourself, and there is a feeling of contact and immediacy. Contact with your environment, with no ghost between it and you. Most of the time, nowadays, this is not so. Exigencies, circumstances, are directing a ghost. The self is in suspense, held back and closed off, just watching. It is surprising, maybe, to be walking so far without getting tired.

It is interesting to see your feet down there, rising and falling. As if it were all on a screen, you are aware that the wood is birch and oak and sweet chestnut, that these are last season's fallen leaves, that these violent, zig-zag gestures of branches must be how old sweet chestnut branches are, that the pale, springy, interwoven beds of this fumitory-like plant under the trees are beds of climbing corydalis, as found in old woods. And that the nightingale's song, when one hears it, will have a throb to it, and will be so strong it will overwhelm the continuous scratchiness of this song, which you hear now, which is that of a whitethroat. And, now you come to listen so carefully, there is another song going on in the background, calling on you to get out of yourself, to open the window a little further, and this one is, in fact, that of a nightingale, just as you were thinking of it. It is far off, but the summons is there, even if you have not managed to respond to it yet.

Sitting in Kris's front room last week, back in Shenstone, I touched my mouth with the side of my forefinger, and the finger was naturally mine. I recognised the contact as being with myself. Identity came completely, for a moment, mouth and finger. I was comfortable about walking in that room, or along the streets in Shenstone. Was that because I had moved about in those places, as myself, for so many years? In Suffolk I am still a guest. It seems as if going will have to follow coming, each time, very soon. The ghost of me collects experience there, but, somehow, dares not take it in hand. It belongs to others, those who have been amongst all that since they were children. My childhood, my first sixty years, are still Midlanded, even though I have no wish to live there again. I walk consolidated down the pavements, past the suburban front gardens, the lilac and laburnum, under the less complex clouds, through the inland weather, the red bricks, the slates. I went into school and Linda gave me a double lesson with the Upper Sixth, doing Tintern Abbey, unprepared, using some photocopies I left on the shelf two years ago. I never had to consider it. It was all there, as engrossing as it used to be. I watched myself perform and I could not feel that it was a performance. Tintern Abbey. These woods. This silent smoke. These green woods. Secret heraldry. A twig is evidently a love bouquet. The apples are a gift. You see them with that sharp look that seems like the cry of a sick man touched on a wound, and there is nothing ghostly.

So, what's to do? Little or nothing. Go out to Hoist Covert again. Even without nightingales. The cloud is low, slate blue, then stained lemon, quickly mutating to a glowing pea-green. There is a thin moon, with Venus, I suppose, just six moon-widths above it. Two curlews are flying, and one of them drops down at a hawk that is flying beneath them, all three birds as black silhouettes. I would not have invented that. Returning through the copse, we meet the robin, which hopped along the path in front of us on the way in. Things don't just disappear. This time he jumps in the twigs and chinks at us as we stand listening... to a tawny owl, kwick, kwick, kwick, then to a nightjar churring some way off over the fields, on the heath. Bird calls from deeper in, from further out. The puddles from last night's rain are easy to step around. The white water tower is dim, like a detailed painting of itself, not quite three dimensional, but certainly not a ghost. Ready to hand? Not quite in touch.

8 June 2002

Here, at last, are the cup-shaped hollows in fine sand, a little smaller than golf balls, that we have been looking for, for twelve months. Under a crumbling crest of low bank which holds up, braced by heather along its top. I now see them easily, because, a few hundred yards away, they have erected a row of wooden posts, with three strings of orange twine along it, to keep us off a similar stretch of bank, and they have put up a notice announcing ant-lions, and even providing a drawing of one and a diagram of how it sits in its pit. I determine to examine the next such bank, outside the enclosure, and, in the shadow of the denser heather overhanging that one, I see more of the depressions at once. When I crouch down and peer, there is one twitch of movement near the bottom of the deepest, under the grains, so I choose that and shove my largest plastic tube in there, half filling it with sand. I have a lump in the tube, like a small piece of defecation, stuck with bits, but moving. Examined, it is a broad, humped body, bristling with dirt, but with a long transparent head and long straight jaws, curved in at their tips. I dump him back in his hollow, after Barbara has had a look. He lies still, but a little digging will restore the original situation. I feel rather like a poacher.

Earlier we found that the sand bank, where there were so many digger wasps nesting two years ago, was similarly fenced off. It also had a notice, announcing the 'bee-wolf' and talking generally of solitary wasps and bees. There were a few orange and black bodied wasps running on the ground, swivelling in the air, just five or six, not the dozens that there used to be. And one large beetle, carrying its body, especially its head, high, and moving faster that a normal ground beetle, with more agility and awareness. It came closer and glinted green, so it was a green tiger beetle, hunting, making moves towards any adjacent insects, forcing them to take off. Later I saw five more of them, one after another, on the path, and each took flight when approached, obviously seeing us well. They always came down again a few yards ahead, and I caught the biggest of them, which did not bother to dodge much, in my tube, where its ferocity was unleashed in jerking and butting. Awareness. Its bulging eyes, dark, in red rims. Red lips, with the long, four-pronged jaws sickling out of them. A blazing green back, petrolic in the sun, and red legs. Yellow spotting on the elytra. Entirely brazen, proud, unafraid, angry. Tigers, lions and wolves, on this walk through the birch woods, over the heath. The ant-lion waits, the tiger beetle rushes about. Sharpness. Piercing. Chopping and sucking. Explosive identities. Competition on the hot dirt.

Last Tuesday we were in Tate Modern looking at Matisse and Picasso. What usually happens with Picasso happened again. I got caught up with later Analytic Cubism and early Synthetic Cubism, and lost interest after that. Here was a Man with a Guitar which I had never seen before, one from the Pompidou Centre, done, I think I remember, in 1910.

The planes remain big, not multiplying as in some hermetic work, yet I am not sure of the disposition of the figure. There are triangles where a couple of heads might be, a few strings near the centre, which might be played, and suggest a placement for the instrument which is still difficult to think through. There are plenty of possible shoulders, forearms, bold planes diagonally across, picked up, lost, re-found further on. Building up the person offers the initial stimulus, but is never completely possible or ever likely to be the main job. Relating all the parts of the shapes to each other, with each other, against each other, in their own terms, is what matters. The process is all discovery. You find how some of it works, and remember how it worked before with other such pictures, and you go in eagerly, getting little shocks as pieces make relations. Why it has to be cubism clarifies again. One has to have flattened planes, with corners, since they give direction, tilt and depth. Only they can do this, can make the three-dimensional structure, can sufficiently resemble each other, slope against each other, be part of a coherent vocabulary which will enable one to feel the scaffolding through. The assembling takes time. I put myself in the corner of the room, next to the picture, so as not to block anyone else who wishes to look at it. Or I go to the middle of the room and catch sights of it through gaps between moving people, who always seem to be gathering there to look at the adjacent pictures. Some people, of course, don't look at pictures at all. They stand there and talk to each other.

The original object being painted, guitar or person, was there to provoke the investigation. It provoked your involvement in the putting together of parts, what you have to do in the world of objects and of experiences, assembling them, to knit it up somehow, giving your attention to the process and to the satisfactions involved in trying to make a whole. The body itself, and its parts, are 'prime objects', basic for relationships which are the basis of every kind of subsequent relationship. That is a remark to be made about this picture, and about everything else one gives attention to. We follow 'keenly' the shifts and alterations made by the artist. Stokes finds the word. 'Keenly'. I find myself more and more keen to keep on looking at this picture. Pears and apples and guitars and the body. Keen. The original sense is 'knowing' or 'skilful'. Dutch for 'bold', 'daring'. Icelandic 'wise', from 'ken'. 'That kenne might alle'. Or causal, 'to make to know', to 'teach' or 'show'.

Last week, on the shingle at the Dingle Marshes, we needed to remember a particular spider in detail. A jumping spider. We had caught one, after half an hour's trying. The difficulty was, as always there, that the spiders saw your hand coming and ducked away down between the flints. There was a population of these spiders, male and female, as well as other species, such as Drassodes. You have to be patient until you catch one, then you can suddenly catch plenty. So I ripped a page out of my diary and scribbled an abdomen, spots on it, a cephalothorax, dashes, a bunch of legs for effect. Very skimpy. When we had the book, later, there it was, Sitticus rupicola, from exactly the angle I had drawn it, mark for mark. 'Shingle beaches in southern and eastern England. Absent or very rare in the region.' We saw it on June 3rd. And it saw us on the same day, its head tilting up, staring with its black, frontal pair of eyes under their thin, ginger eyebrows.

As I write I glance out of the bedroom window, into the garden, enclosed by its considerable hedges, edged by lupins, foxgloves and so on, and there is a big gull standing there, shining white, black backed, yellow legged, smooth, streamlined and out of place. Lesser black back. Come to try for the pink scraps of meat Barbara has put on the bird table, but thwarted by the bird table's roof, which only allows room for a gull's head and neck, forcing it to dance up into the air and lunge, flapping and awkward, to gain the briefest access. It snatches a lump, flops to the grass, and swallows it at once. Starlings come, ignoring the gull, looking small and pointed and rude. They busy about, cleaning up the rest, and the gull leaps up and rows away.

The ant-lion, budging itself in the grains, gaping its colourless fangs. The swift, steady, probing run of the tiger beetle, swerving towards its potential prey, proffering its fangs. The spider's face, and pair of solemn, staring black eyes, well aware of us, swivelling its head. The alien, ice-white, bleak-eyed gull, bouncing up and floundering, dangling its feet. Into each go foreigners from myself, all couth, all uncouth, all partly kenned and certainly, in themselves, keen. Racing to kill, or slouched and ready. A dwarf who is anxious to hide. A great ghost sold short by its greed. Together they seethe together to make up some of a man. Squared off, smoothed, and woven in through loss, retrieval, bewilderment. Set out into fields of deep space. Fetched and disposed and dispatched. All parts of the same wisdom, some of it recognised, much of it new. Bodies that must, somehow, if there is any sense at all, be part of a body. A guess at a mandolin, a meeting with a lord or a lady, people you need to know. In a flick, it discovers its wings and flies, reappearing on the path, yards ahead. The only beetle to take flight readily. Or labours up out of a small space, to get back over the sea. Or waits at the bottom of the hourglass. The hand rests loosely on a ledge, listless, or a string is touched. Momentum becomes pose. Frame that.

6 July 2002

Another evening when the rain has gone and the wind is stilled and all the prickles and blades and stems and twigs and shafts and flags are motionless. As light fails, the overgrown field, across which we go to get to the stile leading into the Mumberry Hills, becomes a quiet blue mist, which is all the speedwell, thick as a crop, with floating white peppering it, which is the campion. Two red deer, not antlered, wade out in the centre, perk up and face us, when they see us coming, and bustle away, this way and that, uncertain that they want to go into cover. Dozens of rabbits suddenly flood across the path. Over the gorse, big beetles drone heavily, five or six of them, one of which I catch in my hand, snatching above my head. It is a summer chafer, with a greasy shine on its elytra, and mottled darker patches on its thorax. Black eyes and black cap to its head. We arrive at the usual spot, facing the two birch bushes which stand out a little into the open heath to the west, and we wait, in a silence where our own stomachs make the most noise.

A nightjar strikes up a churr which lasts for a long time. So they are nearby. It is about ten o'clock. The sky is not blue tonight, nor are there stars or moon. Dabs of dark cloud are more definite than the blur of the overcast beyond them. The sunset seeps through, whitish, with a redder core in a blot of yellow. A nightjar flies close. It is suddenly there, perfectly clear in mid air, silent, then a clap of wings, just the one, before it swerves back behind foliage. For the next twenty minutes it is more or less constantly circling us, following a fixed beat, to our left, from behind, then low over the heather. No more claps. No sound of wings. Often it is directly over us, just a foot or two above us. We see it… see them, if there are two, from all angles, repeatedly, in sharpest focus against the light sky. Long tail, closed or spread. Long, elbowed, slender wings. Short head and neck. The elastic, bouncy flight, of spurts and brakings, a couple of flaps, a pounce forward, long glides with stiff wings outstretched at forty-five degrees, like a paper aeroplane, angling, turning, then into sudden twists and drops. They seem big, elegant, slender, bounding, wafting up, planing down, sweeping low round. Again and again, stretching out the startle. They ignore us, or even use us as markers. Their size and their silence, their closeness and quickness are forcefully lively in the subdued scene. A few bats flicker, with none of the sweep and smooth, hung up sailing of the birds. The nightjars have something of the shock of an alien presence that being near to long, gesturing wings, to essentially airborne birds, brings. Like the swift that thudded into our guttering, into the bottom lip of our pantiles, a few feet from the window out of which I was leaning, last night, leaving its stretched wings sticking out, awkward, before it could pack them away. I could have grabbed it. An assertive, nervous presence under our tiles. Almost an attack on the house. Birds descended from dinosaurs, reptilian still, with stiff feathers and advancing mouths. But fast. Not here. Clap! Here. Thump.

As we drive back there are moths tumbling at the headlights, or coming down on the bright road directly ahead, white, or glowing brown. But the nightjars, their presence, suddenly there after not being there, with no sound of their approach, with the expectation of their being at once gone again. It is the shock of an apparition, which is prolonged and prolonged. That unreflective astonishment. Their posture in the air is a hunch forward, suggested by the blunt head and short neck, the lack of visible beak, and the forward crook of the long wings. Their suspension in the air is as if they were on strings. As if they could pause, if they wished, like a cat walking, half way through a step. Like the end of a line in a Carlos Williams poem. Mysterious. Eerie. So the book says. It is odd to be in such strong expectation of their being here and for their arrival to be so little of an arrival, so much of an already-come. It is because they are so big and so noiseless. Buoyant. Yes. Fingertip control. More hooked than streamlined. They demonstrate apprehension. Breathless. When they churred, they were not here.

27 July 2002

Andy and I drive to Sulmona to see the Sanctuary of Hercules. But it is closed. Above the car park, in the trees, rises Monte Morrone, and a steep path, stepped all the way, leads up through scrub and wood to the church on the site of the cave which was the hermitage of St. Pietro Celestino, before he became Pope, resigned, and was imprisoned. Andy appears to know plenty about him. He gave away power. He ran away when told he had been elected, and was fetched to L'Aquila on an ass, by two knights. After his resignation he tried to escape by boat, but the tides failed and he was caught and held in captivity until he died. I knew none of this. So he was a man who did not want power. He lived here, founded a community here.

The rock face goes on up, in stacks and layers, yellow and coal blue. There are ledges, spurts of plants. The track doubles and re-doubles on itself, fenced with a wooden rail or a stone wall, and supplying the occasional bench. The day is overcast with rain cloud, but there are cracks in this, wells of open sky, circled by white. From one of these a shaft of sun, pale, light-blue, with mauve in it I think, and straight edged, strikes down from above us to way below us, to a spot down on the plain somewhere near the Abbey. The plain of Sulmona. It runs flat away to the mountains, on the summits of which poise the rain clouds. There are straight roads down there, and the city, white and terracotta. There are small fields, belts of trees, factories and playing fields and pools. There must be noise, plenty of it, but almost all of it is lost before it gets to us. There is a motorbike. You can hear a dog bark, and find him out, one of several that are herding a flock of sheep, near to the suburbs, not very pastoral. Up here there are oaks, with finely lobed leaves, pines, cypress and juniper. There are tall, pointed cypresses like those in the background of a Gozzoli. The ground cover is aromatic. There is a fig growing by the iron gate which prevents access to the cave. But we knew it would, like the pagan sanctuary below, be closed. Notices told us so. It is, perhaps, why, for most of the time we spend up here, there is nobody else about. A mullein droops across the path. Two goldfinches cross between trees with yellow on their wings and a quick twittering. On the rocks there are snails with thin elongated corkscrew shells. A bleached, dead millipede snaps in two when I drop him. Celestino, says a notice, heard this silence speak. He heard the rocks talk to the sky. Andy remarks that Douglas Oliver would have liked this man. Andy knew Doug while they both worked at L'Aquila, of course. He is on his mind, and he lit a candle, a fat one that looked like a night-light, for him at Celestino's shrine, yesterday.

What is there here? The wide plain, set in the mountains, under grey clouds. Ladders of light, soft air, remote sounds, ankle-twisting steps, the scent of herbs at every breath. I don't feel a weight of crushing novelty. It is a remarkable place, but it seems that this is not what matters. There is the simple fact that I have not seen most of the world, and I won't, and I am here, surveying the plain of Sulmona. There was someone who was sure he could hear all of this as God speaking. He did not want to be Pope. Others thought he should be. There is room, there is room… this pale ruler of light from the hole in the cloud, which hole then closes like a lense… there is room for conceptions I have not, so far, thought about or talked about, to myself, even. Down the track we go, not speaking a lot. This excursion was not demanded of us. The Sanctuary of Hercules was closed, so we came on up here, knowing the church at the top would be closed too. Celestino, I cannot know him. He was naïve? He granted forgiveness, the Perdonanza, to those who repented and confessed and came to S. Maria di Collemaggio in August, on the 28th to the 29th, vespers to vespers. To accept it meant that you were reborn to unselfishness. Those in authority thought they could use him? He was Pope from August to December. But he was not amenable, tried to escape, was a threat and had to be locked away. I can see the snails on the rocks but not the truth about the politics, nor even am I sure of the facts about the history. I remember my aunt saying, about something doctrinal, 'God won't want to know about that'. Barbara sent a text message to Andy's mobile, which he found as we walked in the main street of Sulmona. She has reached the far point of the journey she is undertaking, the Lake District, and all is going well. I do not have much I want to say to anyone about that. But good. Good. Now I would like to have a look at the aqueduct.

16 October 2002

Overcast and sometimes drizzling. Last night's wind and yesterday's rain have brought down leaves, leaf-stems and codling apples. You pass yourself, rotating upside down in puddles. I write a letter, then extend the walk to the post box by going along Edward's Lane, round again to the village by Walpole Lane. I lean on the railway bridge, above the church, with no hurry to get back, and only a few cars passing.

The wall is capped with curved bricks, coping bricks, I suppose you would call them. Cope. Cape. Cap. Hood. Cloak. Leaves and words. A general tumbling about around what is proper, what might cover the situation. These are red bricks, quite new, that have been well pointed with pale grey mortar in curved trenches between them. There is already moss on them, small tufts with seed capsules. And lichen, whitish, crusty, thin patches with lobed edges. Also powdery white patches shaped like the lichen, which could be vegetative propagation structures. Could be. Names.

A nameless insect, one I know I can't name and won't be able to, walks across the bricks. It is the size and general shape of an aphid, but has, I think, something of a short, pointed tail, and I don't notice any cornicles, nor any wings. It could be a mirid bug. Long, slow-moving, hair-thin legs. Curved, long antennae. A black, shining hump on its back. It walks steadily westwards along the top of the wall. It catches my attention because it moves. When it arrives at a moss tuft it struggles over it, or goes round. But it keeps on going in the same direction along the wall. It avoids craters in the bricks. It crosses mortar without a change of pace. In five minutes it has traversed four bricks. At one moment a diesel train, one coach, roars under the bridge, heading for Halesworth, its black roof is there and gone, under the bridge, the bricks, the insect, in an altogether different world of sound, speed, size, purpose and agitation. The insect is not receptive to it, and never changes its pace. Where is this insect going, and for what? It will take an hour to cross the rest of this bridge and make it to the hedge, and by then it will be dusk. It cannot ever have been over there before, or have any sort of home or destination over there. If it rains it will be knocked off. When it is dark… will it still walk on? It is the end of the season. There is nothing for it to look forward to. It will never be seen by anyone who has words again. And another insect, a minute one shaped like a spring-tail, too small to see in any detail, small even in comparison with the first one, hurries past it, missing it by a fraction, not meeting it, moving much more quickly, with invisible legs, as if it were sliding completely smoothly over the surface. But this one is not going in one direction, but rather gives the impression of passionately searching in all directions. It has soon vanished. A tiny, reflected light shines from the sky on the polished hump of the first insect, still heaving along, leg after leg, each leg picked up, advanced, set down.

How much is there to understand? Is this taking place in a sort of sub-zone, where there is nothing to know about function, purpose, the end of journeying, the getting of food, warmth, the arrival at a crevice to have a home in? I note, afterwards, in a book, that there is a bug called Mecomma ambulans. It isn't this one, though its female is a little like it. But—ambulans. That is what there is to be said about it. On a journey, with no intention. Mindlessly leg after leg, tilting, slightly, the reflection it is getting from the October sky, from the weather which is coming in over this wide landscape off the sea. On a bridge coping, with trains going north or south under it, while it goes west, as if heading for Walpole, Bury St. Edmunds, Cambridge, the Midlands, Wales. This was once the road that came from Dunwich and went to Bury. It would take lifetimes to get to the next house. The crashing speed of the train under it boggles all its possible criteria, sets its whole life into absurdity.

I jump with shock as a footfall sounds behind me. It is a young man with two dogs, one of which barks at my sudden movement. I apologise, for some reason... for being there for no reason. He smiles and grunts and hauls the dogs on... towards Walpole.

I go home and pull out some books, wondering if you can have a coping brick as well as a coping stone. Lichens of Great Britain. Guide to Insects. So. A piece of live stuff. Ambulans. If I took a torch and went back I might find it, maybe at rest now it is dark. That is... stopped. With no supper, surely. Not a friend in sight. Colder now, but still not raining. Learning for Life is the title of a booklet on the table.

15 November 2002

It is probably 404 years since Hamlet first said, 'The rest is silence'. I woke up in the small hours thinking this, without doing the sum but feeling the length of time, and, most vividly, how every moment since had been, has been, filled with particulars. For instance, the nose of an aardvark. The nostrils and the little mobile mouth on the end of the snout. And the hardness of sinew and flesh of the snout itself, and the fur on it. I think this first came because it is an image of purpose directed to a point, the mouth. But it was followed at once by the sense of touching the snout, patting it as one would the nose of a horse, and the hardness and short furriness of it, if one did that. Its existence under one's hand. Other notions poured in after this, also particular. The lines of the 60s pop song, 'At half past ten in the morning, she took me by surprise.' Maybe I am misremembering that. But it came with the pleasure of such an unlikely time of day for falling in love, for finding, suddenly, a particular person to be amazing. Not in the evening but in the rush of the day getting itself underway. There were others, all in a hurried tumble, but half past ten in the morning and the nose of an aardvark, the pale fur on it, buff or greyish, and no softness in the flesh and bone under it... And all these specifics existing in a time after Hamlet first said his line, and thus released that realization, in those words, in that pun on 'rest', especially in its most negative sense, which seemed to be, simply, in the dark in the bathroom last night, all these specifics devoid of any consequences, each just itself, for no purpose. No more words about any of them. To fit them into any scheme instantly seemed to melt them into a phoney glamour, make them part of a poor sort of drama, the sort that an audience at a reading of an autobiography would enjoy, smiling and nodding and exclaiming that the writing was beautiful, with wonderful imagery. I remember the light from the streetlamp coming through the open bathroom door onto the black and white diamonds of the bathroom floor, dimly, with myself standing further in, looking back, southwards, at the soft, exact glow on this floor, on these big, dim diamonds. Specifically there, this floor, also, long after Hamlet had proposed that silence, this silence, in the bathroom. And all the particulars, bobbing up alongside each other, though they could have been entrancing, distinctive and thrilling in their differences, were, instead, rather sickening in their rush and noiseless clamour, though to deal with this by seeing them smoothed out into some sort of consequential sequence, set, maybe, into a meaningful biography, seemed a capitulation, not worthy of the hard forehead of the aardvark under its thin skin, or the soft glossiness of the streetlamp's light on the diamond tiles, however fretful the huge pile of these particulars might be. I had a notion of giving a reading where, to begin it, I stunned an audience with the full sense of this before I began the poems, then dropped those into a shocked hush, a vibrating emptiness. And the poems themselves would not be, as it were, 'treatment' to give one a sense of having dealt with anything by writing about it, smoothing it down. No soothing the aardvark, or the rest of all the rest since 1598, or 1601, whenever a mouth first opened on those words.

But these particulars must have come from somewhere? From walking past North Valley farm where they are keeping horses. Not very convincing. From the toughness of the body of Miff the terrier we looked after overnight for Julia and Herman, the niftiness of her body, the tilt of her head when she goes quiet and thinks. And a tape of the song I was playing two days ago. That is easy. Fused with other particular hearings of such songs. The first time I heard 'All Shook Up', on a Black Box record player of polished, expensive looking wood, by the French windows with the light coming in through them into the back of the room. The rubber mat, red, that the record sat on, and the click of the machine's metal arm dropping the record into place. Someone's claim that this was the greatest piece of rock and roll ever. Someone making that claim. The manic, snagged onto a sunny morning set into half past tens and sunlight on sideboard and record player, with its moving parts, the contact of a needle on vinyl, and the loud pressure, not quite silence, waiting for the first note. All of it, very specific but gone, unsmoothed, jagged, with the rest, into silence, as it was, last night, in the small hours. All shook up. How do you spell it? 'Aardvark'.

22 April 2003

Maybe the orchids are beginning in Reydon Wood, so Barbara and I go there at midday. The bluebells are half open, pooling off amongst the trees. There are clumps of primroses in the rides, and also in shadier places. Papery and throated with yolk. Cool leaves pushing between packed flowers. Celandine is even more common, their greasy petals turning silver as they reflect sky. Wet, where the primroses are dry. Darker green and darker yellow. There are tight-set beds of ground-ivy, the frills of blue petals protruding between layers of toothed leaves. Greater stitchwort by the path that leads us in. Wild strawberry flowers more thinly spread. Violets. The cunning of richness which sets blues amongst greens, close to some selected white companions.

There are orchids, a few, not wide open yet, their snakes' heads ducking down under a cobra-hood spur, and a loose lower jaw hanging agape. Crimson purple. Early purple. The undeveloped ones have no spots on the leaves, but one group, this time fully open, showing the pale patch and spots on their tongues, the lip having swollen and curved over at its edges, are boldly spotted, the spots running along the leaves, not transversely as in the named 'spotted' species. Mascula, then. Early purples indeed.

Robins sing cold notes. Blackbirds make it warmer. Then there is something more than these. Another order of singing altogether. A throatiness and volume. One envisages bubbles in thicker liquid. There are crescendos as a single note is repeated. A stony rattling. And jug, jug, jug. There is one nightingale singing from the brushwood at the edge of the tall trees, beyond the bluebells and the stacked logs. We move back and forth on the path, staring into the thicket, and, this time, we see him, high on a hazel bush. The leaves are new green, and only sprinkled thinly in the air, as little sheaves of ribs that are only now opening. The bird is not thrush sized. It has a chestnut rump, is hopping high there, and then stays, sideways, behind a spray. You can see his gentle eye, with the pale ring round it, and the thin beak opening and closing round the song. He lets a run of it go, full tilt, then pauses as if he might stop and slip away, because he does not fancy being watched. A very highly charged pause. Then more and more song. Other birds pass through. Some long-tailed tits, one of which stops to preen, grey and pink and black, the long tail curved up as it nibbles itself. There is much space in the wood, up there, under the canopy, where two chaffinches are sweeping about. A treecreeper, cream and brown, maculated, with thin eye-stripe and curved bill, all shown to us clearly, moves up a smooth trunk. A chiffchaff in the hedge is watching us and calling out at the same time. A ragged dark-brown hare comes towards us along a path through the wheat field beyond the hedge, then turns and lollops away. White ears with black tips. And a big, shining eye.

These are the orchids in Hamlet, the long purples, the 'dead man's fingers', the 'priest's pintles', with two tubers, one evacuating its goodness into the present growth, the other filling up for next year. Orkhis. Testicle. The 'satyr plant' which causes 'great heat and giveth lust', from the swelling testicle, and restraint from the slack one. So says Grigson. Thessaly in Suffolk. Like this since the Middle Ages, when they began to coppice this place. The celandine tubers suggest the teats of a cow. The petals suggest butter and produce the tide of cream in the udder. The root, four bulbs, was hung in the byre in the Highlands and Islands. Butter, milk and sperm. And the starry primrose, with the strong 'swell' given by the 'deeper yellow in the middle' as Hopkins saw, in 1871, the same year when he wrote about the bluebells, whose stalks, rubbed together in a bunch, click, making a sound like 'a hurdle strained by leaning against' as they jostle in your hand. A never-to-be-forgotten passage, to recall you to the quality of life whenever you feel there is not much to it. The bluebell stems, bunched in your fist, and clicking. To get it true and at the same time find it astonishing. Bluebells and the orchids share names, Grigson notes. Both are Snake's Flower, Cuckoo-Flower, Crowtoes, Granfer Griggles. Spring juices. Both are on the Unicorn Tapestries, on the climactic one celebrating marriage. Viola odorata, Vinca minor, Arum maculatum, Orchis mascula. And bluebell. The unicorn is tied to the pomegranate tree. A wood full of tubers. Roots to make glue, and slime on the roots. And then, the bitter touch to give an edge to the bubbling of the nightingale's song, a bit of a sharp rattle, the ground ivy, ale-hoof, to make beer. The blue tongue between the sharp green teeth. And what of 'grig'? A 'small, lively eel', Skeat says. Or, not connected with this, a 'cricket', probably because of the sharp noise, 'crick'. Bluebell stems crick as they wriggle. Or an eel in your trousers. What of 'griggles'? Apples left on the tree, too small to be worth picking. To go 'griggling' is to collect those. Eels and apples. Come home with those, then, found in the wood.

4.30. I have just come back from an hour or more on the Rock of the Cross, picking the tracks through the wood easily this time, no mistakes. There are two peregrines, though I only saw them both at the same time once, when they flew close together and might have touched. The rest of the time it was the male, I presume, doing his circuits of the space at the junction of the valleys and coming back to his perch on a trunk, clear of vegetation, jutting from a ledge across a cleft in the buttress of bare limestone next to the Rock where I was. Or, twice, he settled for a perch on the shelf, a little further off. Most of the time he kept up his calling. It was like a brake that is catching on a car's wheel, as the car comes fast downhill, a run of such sounds, from nine up to twenty. Or maybe like a chicken's cluck, more annoyed than satisfied. Cacking. He kept it going while he was doing his circuits in the air, and while he perched. As he flew up at the rock face, either to perch or to spin over and drop out again into the valley, his voice swelled and took on a loud echo from the cliff he was approaching. Often his turns brought him close to me so I could see his barred under parts with the two yellow legs laid back flat, his moustache, smart on his white cheek, his yellow bill, black head, barred tail, his rump, greyer than the rest of his upper parts, and the lightest feathers on the leading edge of the wing, at the base of the primaries. Sometimes he went high above me, each circle taking him into the sun, where I could not follow him though he was still calling and gliding up there, smoothly curving round. When he was below me, against the woods and slopes, seen through binoculars, he was hard to keep up with, but, after a while, I came to trust that I would find him again.

In the village opposite me there were a couple of houses, with thirteen terraces below them, then forty or more above them, mounting to the buildings higher up. In the lower terraces, a man in a red cap was working with a hoe, carrying a white plastic bucket, or sitting on a step, having a cigarette. A white-haired woman worked near him, rolling up some netting. To their right, an older man in a blue shirt leant on a staff and there were thirty goats around him, one or two dark brown, most of them cream, heads down, dangling long, pendulous ears. They were spread out in the shade under some trees. The old man leaned on his staff, and, maybe, watched the falcon cross over his head. Looking for Icarus. There was a further village, over the shoulder of the mountain, with a church, then more mountains, silver blue, and the Argentina running off along their feet beside the main road, on which was the minute figure of a man on a motor bike shooting along. To my right, the wooded valley under the peregrine's rock had a river in it, which I could hear, and find a small glimpse of, between branches. The sky clouded and light altered. The perching place was brimmed with bright oak and dark olives. The slab I was on protruded over deep space so that, whenever I stood up on it, I was aware of the proximity of its edge and the emptiness of the drop, so much so that I wobbled, made sure of my foothold, and often stepped back.

Next morning, 6th May, and the peregrine is overhead, calling continuously, maybe irritated by my presence. It makes off towards the woods and is lost against the trees. Later, there it is again, very high up, still calling, and attacking a golden eagle, which flinches away from its stoop, and circles higher until it is only a speck against small white clouds, disappearing, at last, against the blue. There was a second eagle, smaller, nearby when the peregrine first attacked, but I lost track of that one when I followed the bigger one up and up.

Back from the Rock at sunset, fetched by Herman. The sun an inch above the mountain tops in front, my mind's eye full of falcon. Seeing it curve near its clay and cream cliff face, then closer, chittering all the time. The breast, tail, face, beak, legs, and with more glamour when the sun struck on the downbeat of the wings.

Then two spiders, both on the Rock itself, alongside me. A small jumping spider that is bouncing frantically from side to side when it sees my hand. It is gold-green, iridescent, velvety. It has dark palps and eyes and legs, and is a male. Heliophanus tribulosus. Then an equally minute crab spider, running fast. Long black legs at the front, pairs further back colourless. A white mask over its eyes. Misumena vatia, male. I think. Both on the warm rock, here with the scent of thyme and lovage. I catch them very carefully, not moving myself close to the edge.

Such preciousness. Such a precise clamouring. Clarity. Nitidus. Tidy. The bird over there and the spiders here. Herman and Miffy the dog arrive, and Miffy runs immediately to the very edge and looks directly down over it.

17 July 2003

Ripon Cathedral. Wilfrid's Crypt. Tight passages lead down to this small cell. It has one adornment only. Quite high on the east wall there is a 14th century alabaster panel of the Resurrection. It is frightening, energetic caricature. Christ strides, with a leap, out of the tomb. His right leg is stretched out spectacularly long and thin. His hand is thrown up, giving the two finger blessing, the other fingers curled up. His body is thin, the ribcage bulging like a pair of swung breasts. The soldiers, painted in red and blue garments, with black plate armour, gloves, pointed helmets and solid gorgets, are, I take it, impossibly asleep in these lunatic attitudes, though one appears to be sleeping with his eyes open, glazed and goggling up into space. This is the man on the right, sitting upright, with his head tilted back, resting against his spear. Christ lands on the one who is propped on his elbow at the base of the tomb. The third is behind the tomb, slumping forward. None of them, of course, see Christ, who blasts out of death within inches of them. Christ is white as a spider, nearly a cadaver. Electrifying. Not one atom of beauty in the whole piece. An irrepressible, jumping man, come to shock the living daylights out of you. The soldiers are left as stultified fools. The white pennon flickers with its red cross on Christ's staff. Maybe someone knocked up a flag while in Hell, or it was providentially there in a banner-stave locker just inside the doors. Anyway, the little, coloured, violent panel is the superb focus in this blank, ancient cellar, that smells of dust.

Upstairs, in the choir, are the misericords, each in its wedge under its shelf, each tilted into flattened perspective, each cut by a master. Packed in and rhythmic. Samson carries the doors. A griffin seizes a rabbit while the rump of a second rabbit is vanishing down a burrow. A fox carries a goose over its shoulder, while another preaches in a pulpit. There are two blemyae as supporters, one with a pudding-basin hat, and these are either side of the carrying of the gigantic bunch of grapes. Antelopes have notched horns, used as saws to prune out sins. The owl is up the corner, in the darkest seat, as he always is. A funeral is going on, so we have to leave and come back later. Notch. Groove. Bulge. Bump. Bunch. Bag. Block. Burrow. Fold. Crease. Polish. These misericords master an idiom and their material, unrivalled by the stone carving we came to see. They are difficult to look at in this gloom. You have to peer down at them from out of the row of seats in front. But they are worth this journey on their own. What about those two blunt bears, wound about with vines? Snouts and backs and paws and bunches of grapes. Twisted angles, broadened backs, nothing cut to be thin. The green man is upside down, spewing the thicket upwards. These are as accomplished as those in Norwich or Lincoln. Their oddities are mainstream. Jonah is thrown overboard, or he rises out of the whale's mouth close inshore, where rounded trees grow to the water's edge. You look down into a tilting ship which is like a basket crammed with torsos, the crow's nest as the handle. Such constrained fields of action under the seats. The world full of many of the usual monsters, but each done so it is fully turned on, it wakes you up, demands your touch, strains your eyesight into the shadows so you don't miss any part of a body, a tendril, the turn of a head, a leering mouth. And they are joyful because they are brilliant. The actual funeral is still in process. Black suited men are carrying the coffin, slowly. A quiet voice comes over the speakers, talking of the defeat of death, 'neither height nor depth'.

23 August 2003

As I came back up the garden, I sat down on the bench, and stayed there a couple of hours. Barbara was in the attic with the computer, the roof window by her open, the electric light in there strengthening during those hours, from invisible, to a suggestion, to gold in a cave. There was continuous cloud crossing, with blue gaps paling between. Metal grey. Lead silver. With darker whiffs. At first there were touches of citrine, not brown, not yellow, not orange... which chilled and disappeared. There was a small star, which I thought was a satellite because it was moving, but this movement was transferred from the clouds, as I realised when the star reappeared in the same place later. No swifts. No sparrows. No starlings. The raucous bird life has moved away from the garden, to Africa or into the fields and marshes. House martins still, high, in a group, like swifts but slower, gentler, quieter. Thirty or so of them. They vanish as darkness comes.

A bird appears, suddenly, in the dusk, on the clothesline, seated there unrocking, instantly solidly set. Then it hops onto the line post, that branch of yew that we use as such. A robin. It gives a short burst of song in the dark. Another is on the grass, a dim lump which flurries off. I can hear short songs and brief calls from the oak. A dragonfly is passing and re-passing along the hedges, right up to the darkness. Moths close to my face. Bats, quickly. A few gulls, in formation, high, their wing beats not seeming enough to keep them suspended, let alone to drive them so firmly ahead. I stand up to go in and wash up, which I had intended to do two hours ago. I was wondering if I would sense the universe as an entity, silver and citrine and grey, spread softly around through complexity, spaced wide but filled with the body of evening air very slightly moving, holding lively items that are about their own businesses yet all with each other. Some entity which mattered in its not, probably, mattering too much. I had no feeling of my heart beating, regularly or not. I rested my chin on my hands, on the table, and looked at the bleached grass, flattened, intricate, a basis, between my feet, then back up at the scene in front... hedge, teasels, lychnis, blanching blue thistles, chicory stems and screws of their flower heads, corrugated roofs of sheds next door, house roofs beyond down in the village. Detail in layers, with illumination fading, reds going black, blues going white, fading and graduating itself perfectly in degrees of distance, making no fuss. A few plants, which I had watered, standing their leaves up eagerly. The rest eking it out, with no rain expected, yet again, for several days. A robin is singing in the dark garden.

13 October 2003

To the Hen Reed Beds this morning, on impulse, leaving the house cleaning half done. In the creek there was a seal which had caught a big fish, the size of a slab-filling salmon. The seal's head, and its forepaws, holding the fish head uppermost, rose above the surface of little waves which were running inland as small pyramids with sparkles of clear bubbles threading over their tips, all travelling briskly. The fish's mouth was a round hole. Its stomach was bitten out and bloody. The seal's nostrils opened and closed, its black eyes were spectacled by pale fur, its white whiskers stiff and hard, its fur glued down, wet and shining. It was often on its back, holding the fish up to its chin, biting out pieces of silver and pink. Then it would sink under for a time and rise again, always head and forepaws only, in the same place, in spite of the tide. It was watching us. We were only ten yards from it, sitting on the bank, our binoculars rising and falling. A kestrel overhead, swept round by the wind, chestnut, cream and black spotted.

Cold fish in your mouth. Raw. Estuary water lapping inside your cheeks, running through your lips, tinctured with cold blood. How do I stand towards this? An episode that was protracted long enough for some contemplation, so that the creature was as if a dog, made familiar, as if patted, almost smelled. Drenched fur greased down on the globe of the skull. Eyeballs in sockets, sending us their regards. The head slipping under. The fish more damaged, nearly bitten through, when it emerged again, to be examined and juggled. Then… no fish. Just the seal's face, thrown up as when someone lies comfortably over to swim on his back. Leaving at last into the chopping water down the way of the sun, blinding us.

I assume the seal recalls little of this, is enclosed by chilly water somewhere back out in the estuary, feeling well fed, maybe with a taste still in its mouth diluted by all that passing salty liquid. I assume it knows, mostly, only what it is like to be immediately in contact with experience. But even fish, so it has been proved, remember for quite some time. That fish had a tragic mask, sure enough, a round open mouth, gills, slits running together above its pale throat. Silver-grey scales on its back. A ragged tail fin and other fins spiking out, looking desperate. Swallowed now, by seal and time. Sealed. Only I continue to make a meal of it. On the front lawn there is a yellow spray of fallen ash, laid out neat and intricate, as if on display, and it at once suggests the margin decoration in some mediaeval manuscript. Someone looking at plants six hundred years ago, to copy them, reproduce them, carve them. The leaf carving in the Chapter House at Southwell Minster. Records of the particular, not stylised, very sharply registered. Accuracy, detail and, I suppose, if not really so wonderful, maybe just so many more observed facts. That loneliness of all the facts. I recall that pretty soon after seeing the seal's head revolving in the water, pretty soon after the surprise of realising what it was that I was looking at, pretty soon after clearly seeing the close details of the features of seal and fish, I was thinking it was time to be moving back to the car… while at the same time supposing I ought to stay and see the detail out, in case there was something else, something more, a development, another angle. The creature in the water, swimming close, demonstrating how to eat, what eating is. Meeting us, glancing at us with some sort of acknowledgement. The lips mumbling about the nasty snags of bones. Professionalism staring calmly along its snout. The side of the bottom jaw of a lion as it rolls its head over to one side to get purchase on a joint of meat, in some zoo, some other time. I don't think I was waiting for the seal to speak.

27 November 2003

A day of gale force wind and rain which settled towards dark and since then, yesterday and today, relative calm. More than that, complete calm this afternoon and evening. Suspended, so it feels, on a precarious edge of total stillness which must be soon to slide into more storm. Twigs don't move against the sky. Cloud is brushed out fine and filmy from the south, from the orange lower sky, with slips of it charged with burning chrome-orange, almost white. Smooth dove-grey masses, slightly plummy. The top of the sky is cerulean, yet chilled and sharp in impact. The heather on Dunwich Heath is quiet raw-umber, creamed with brown milk. The low sun puts the orange across it onto the trunks of the birches. Thin strips of short grass by the paths are emerald. The distance, beyond Minsmere scrape and including Sizewell, block and dome, seems altogether toned down so that it stands well back, ghosted.

We walked on the beach and the sea was an astonishment. Flat. Polished smooth right out to a thin darker strip at the horizon. The flatness was electrified and impossible in its brightness, the shadows on the sides of the small wavelets an artificial cobalt with purple in it, and a little rosiness on the top of the surge. But, to so far out, flat, shining silver like cellophane or silk. On the far rim of the bright area were five or six swimming birds, heads tilted up, white necks and sides—red-throated divers. They dive, vanishing into the smooth, solid gleam. They appear again, beaks up-tilted, bodies low, white glinting. Either there or not there. No waves to conceal them. Of course one can hear the rush, steadily, not emphatically, from the tide line, but the level, shining, brilliant surface and the birds there, not there… the implication is a surprised silence. Existing and not existing closed with each other with no fuss. Some sort of demonstration of how much there is in so very little. No more than this—a swimming bird with a few distinctive features, offshore, on the rim of the brilliance, proud and sleek. Then gone. To come back not quite predictably, but clear and neat, far out, just within recognition. The one further in, white faced, blacker, is a cormorant. There are some gulls. Their white looks old against the huge gleam of the sea. They turn and flap as little matt patches on the expanse, the great swash of oiled, luscious, unnaturally unbroken ocean.

The child whose only use of his toys was to play 'Gone' with them, used to throw his wooden reel, on the end of its piece of string, into his cot so that it disappeared, then pull it back into sight and shout 'Da'. The complete game of disappearance and return. To let mother go away and feel that she will come back.

We turn inland and on a birch against the sky, on the top branches, three stumpy, plump sparrow-like birds, just larger than sparrows, sit firm and upright. One snaps its bill at the tip of a twig. Their breasts glow rosy and they fly off, their flight very undulating. Surely the crossbills, here as they were last week. Snap on the twig. Da.

21 December 2003

For days now a gale and snow have been predicted to arrive from the north on a sudden switch of wind direction, which will drive down the coast. We fetched Eric from Stowmarket station yesterday. There were sudden, heavy rainstorms, but still coming from the southwest. Clouds of a surprising blackness and solidity, worked up with sulphurous yellow underneath, suddenly cleared as night fell, drawing off with hard edges and speeding away, baring a blaring blue-white sky. We pulled into the Victoria at Earl Soham on our way home, to set the holiday on its way. There was a fire in that peculiar fireplace in between the two rooms, with the picture of Queen Victoria, leaning on her elbow, over it. A couple of people were eating. Then four musicians came bundling in, with a tuba, a euphonium and two cornets. They played carols from the Salvation Army Brass Band Selection, just to us, because the others had finished their meal and gone, quickly, because their dog did not like the music. In the Deep Midwinter, Once in Royal David's City, played quite softly in the enclosed space, trembling the tight volume of air. Christmas. Snow on snow. Long ago. A sweet tearfulness, as if a neglected door were standing open, to your surprise, and a very well-known path was immediately outside and would be glad to be trodden on again. The chill in my stomach was massaged away by the vibration of the tuba's notes.

Yesterday Robert came and we watched fourteen white sanderling run, and stop, and run on the tide line and on the edge of the fresh water at Benacre.

Stumps of grey trees stuck out of the mud because the Broad has almost drained into the sea, through the narrow strip of beach. Two goldeneye found a depth they could dive into. We drove to Minsmere to be at the Island Mere at dusk. The sun was lowering in front of us, of course, blinding out some of the surface, laying it down as flat gold, into which the silhouettes of coot and goldeneye and scaup humped over and slipped down without splashing. Bewick's swans made a murmuring. A pair of marsh harriers and a barn owl were in the middle distance, in front of Sizewell and the ruined chapel. Clarity and stillness, with the promised storms and snow a day away.

In the evening we watched a compilation of the Falstaff scenes from the three Henry plays, done by Circle 67 Players in the Cut at Halesworth. They unwound slowly but carefully, so that I began to be reminded. Mistress Quickly's fumbling of the dying man, upwards from his feet, all cold as any stone, as he subsides into the truth of himself, and she reaches the false, cold staff as opposed to the hot spur. The dying king's delight that Hal can speak so well to excuse himself for taking the crown off the pillow, which surely does not mean he believes Hal is telling the truth, merely that he is gratified to find Hal such an excellent man of words. Which is part of an answer to Falstaff's attack on words, the word 'honour' in particular, as mere 'air'. Words, in spite of facts. Hamlet swearing that he really can rant, and will eat crocodiles to prove he loved Ophelia. Which gives you an oath to stand by, a love you have at least sworn by, so that you have somewhere to be when you have your chance to 'say one' and make the sword's point. 'I better brook the loss of brittle life than those proud honours thou hast won of me.' Years ago Geoff and I were sitting by our gas fire in Jesus sorting it out and believing that nobody else had quite got the hang of it as well as we were doing, that it all knitted together as we knew it did that night, not a phrase was superfluous, not an image but was working. And Brockbank listening to it, eyes glaring, cigarette sparking, in the supervision at the end of each week. In Halesworth, tonight, I feel the pressing importance of all of that, even in the fragments we are being given. An occasional gust of wind shakes the doors, but the words are audible and the coming storm forgotten.

On Tuesday it does not come, not during daylight hours. But by 10 pm the road is filmed with small flakes, descending at a steep angle, and the weather warnings are for tomorrow. There is something to be endured. Ruth and

Tom should arrive then. We are looking after next door's hens. I hear Barbara fetching a spade from the shed, preparing a big tray in case we have to feed them inside their hut. 15 cm forecast in Norfolk. A last look out of the front bedroom window. Scarcely any is falling, but the two lamps opposite show how sticky the dusting that has come down is. It caps the fence posts, coats one side of trunks, and the telegraph pole up to its top. It has plastered the cars parked opposite us, under the hedge, so that windows are continuous sheets with the doors. Eager weather. Avid to arrive and happen. We deserve it. We have done something wrong. The nine men's morris is filled up with mud. There is a repertoire which likes us to worry, because we have stirred it up when there was no need for that. When we wake up, when we draw the curtains, will there be traffic passing? Or muffle? White light on the ceiling?

Nothing very passionate. 8 am. No digging out of chickens. The snow has dropped from trunks and poles. Cars slosh by. Only roofs and sheltered lawns are white. A hedge sparrow is creeping under the hornbeams and maple. Birds have their courses, trajectories, corners to search into. They are already far on, stringing their day together, stepping on dead leaves in crystalline snow, on the taut, brittle surfaces packed about by the little clusters of melting glass. Scratching and touching and tapping sounds, if you were down in the hedge. More snow comes. We begin a snowman on the back lawn and give him stone eyes. After dark, he freezes. He is a presence in the garden. The aura of a manikin. He is the owner. With the back door light and kitchen lights off, I can't see him from the bedroom window, only the track of bared grass where his body rolled, leading off to where he must be. He will sink away, dirtied, still a collapsing lump when the rest of the snow has gone. What has he to accuse me of? Making him stand when there was no need for it? He is the man, with an unnaturally large head, who stares up the side of the house, waiting. Warding? A sentinel, ever since I gave him a head. One who is awake. Who takes his stand, for a time, on the edge of the dark. I made him fold his arms and hold his face up on a stiff, thick neck. He will be there when Tom and Ruth come to the door.

5.30 pm on Monday, 22nd December, 2003. I will never be here again, and the snowman says so. I go out and stick a garden cane under his folded arms, at a tilt, and tie a stiff, frozen rag to its tip. Give him a flag.

8 April 2004

At ten o'clock on Thursday night we are walking back through the Campo Santo Stefano when a young woman, in a long, light coat, and with dark hair in a swatch falling over her shoulder, begins to sing Verdi, Schubert, Puccini, in an effortless mezzo-soprano, accompanied by a recorded orchestra, playing quietly. She stands under a lamppost with three lights at the east end of the Palazzo Loredan. There are four of these lampposts down either side of the Campo, and not many other lights, even in windows. She has placed a hat on the ground a dozen paces in front of her.

At first, there are only six or seven of us brought to a halt, in pairs or singly. The blanched, frock-coated, bearded man, raised well above us, is Nicolò Tommaseo, the letters of his name too shallowly cut to be readable in the gloom. The paving takes the lights across it and has a silkiness. The moon is very bright, not quite full, and the sky is disclosed, as in no other city I know, so you can see the stars, and particularly one fierce planet. The people who have stopped stand on their shadows. There is a man in a Stetson, a woman in a trouser suit, a youth zipped in leather. He is chewing gum. He stays a long time and stands out at the front of us, looking hard at the singer. Two dogs scamper about, chasing and rollicking, one of them long-haired, black and white, shaggy and effortful, the other a black lurcher, all elastic. Their claws patter on the stone. More people arrive suddenly as the audience leaves the concert at S. Vitale. The half-circle of listeners grows to sixty or so. She stands straight, or leans forward slightly, with a book in her hands. After each song she stoops to her recording equipment to choose the next one. Most people who were in the initial, small group, have stepped forward by now and dropped money in the hat. There are rounds of applause, echoing for a second after each song. Windows, in rows, are all attention. Barbara sits on the step of a marble wellhead. Some of the S. Vitale audience are young Americans and they are talking loudly as they approach in spite of the silent crowd ahead of them. They notice nothing until they are vigorously shushed by several people. A boy mocks the singer's voice as he approaches, passes in silence, then renews the mockery, from the darkness, when he is further off again. She comes in often at barely a whisper, and surges without a wobble. She fills the square and is with you round the corner, as if she were there too, coming from the opposite direction. Ivy tendrils loop down from a window box, rigid and listening. Their shadows repeat them, exactly, on the wall behind, with no mistakes. She stands silent for quite long moments, waiting for her entry. One older woman is not to be a part of it. She lowers her chin and strides past, close by, never looking or hesitating. A young man advances, talking into his mobile phone. The dogs are amongst the legs of the crowd, agile, concerned with each other's sexiness. Couples hold hands. S. Stefano itself is enormous and not missing much. The voice is making the notes, but it is also waiting for each of them, catching it cleanly. A campo full of standing people, in attitudes, as if they were in a picture by Carpaccio. But she sang beyond the genius of the dogs. They were wholly body, fluttering their empty ears. Inhuman, veritable dogs.

15 June 2004

On a cream painted wall here is a square of sunlight filled with boiling shadows, come in through the window glass, cast by the leaves outside which are blown in a noiseless breeze. Like what? Fingerprints dabbled in shining gelatine, with darker uncertainties moving under them. Uncertainties, out of focus, held in lesions of brightness which are evident only when ripples of shadow pass beneath them. The glass must be old, thick, unevenly dimpled. Worries discover blazing shapes. Sometimes the shadows clarify, here and there, as thin but always partly disconnected lines. They must come from twigs which are being swept across outside. They throw out little attempts, which vanish almost immediately, doused in the crystal insistencies. Sometimes a blot stabs down fingers, as if playing on piano keys through a storm of flames. In ten minutes the square has moved right off the wall onto a chest of drawers, painted a matt Air Force blue. On this stands, in calm light, an earthenware pot, varnished. Look again. Earthenware, varnished, steady, containing a huge lily, its spades of thick rubbery leaves curving down so that one of them, moments ago, cast a perfectly definite composed shadow of itself into the seething square, though that has now moved on, in transit. One shadow. Accurate and hard-line. On the wall over all this there is a photograph of a group of people, which shows seated women, a row of pale blouses, and, above them, five men in dark suits, who stand with their heads exactly level, like a firing squad of well-matched personnel, looking straight at you, clear of the volley of inaudible popping and burning in the square which is well down below.

115

Peter and Beryl left, at half-past ten last night, with their packs on their backs, to walk in the Pyrenees. It is now eight a.m. and this is their front bedroom in Sturton Street. They won't have slept. They will be on the plane for Toulouse, or beyond that, on a train. This morning, later, Peter will be in the cave at Niaux, seeing cave art, painted and engraved. He will not be seeing this crystal blot moving sideways across the chest of drawers, holding its small tides of cohesions and incohesions washing back and forth inside it, losing and refinding references to what must be a coherent tree outside, over the street. Now a round wooden knob on the top drawer, painted blue as the rest, is included in the screen of activity, but with a thin moon of intense undisturbed shadow enclosing its left side. Some clear astronomy. I have here, in this room with me, the certainty of things to which I give extended close attention. My subjective life, and any of the increasingly more objective overviews which can oversee it and reduce it to absurdity, melt together in the square of sunlight, pinch together on the knob, cup together round the earthenware pot, palm themselves together, a pair of hands, under the motionless lily leaves. My minute friends, at an enormous distance from me, are out of it, so it seems, crossing under astronomy, over geography, making time, pin-pointed, dumbfounded in prehistory and history and blanked out of this, now, where I am and they are not. What conclusions are there to be had watching them as if from outer space, or from this immediacy? Here, from the warmth of the morning air in their house, with their lily in its pot and, look, a candle next to that on their chest of drawers, unlit of course, stuck in a low pewter candlestick, its wax the colour of old bone and totally still, as if it had been there, put in its place by a Magdalenian. That fixture, next to that of the dusty, dusty dark green lily leaves. I see their importance and give what I have to it, so that it does not, yet, shrink away. There is the seething, trapped in the square. All other points of view, systems, seethe together and blink out in this present seething. Coincide. But somewhere, gone, Peter and Beryl are managing, lost in themselves, in the mountain country, in the cave, unobtainable. But surely, surely not. They are somewhere here too, somewhere about here in what does not appear at the edges of the leaves, what does not flare off the wick of the candle. It is good to be talking to them.

17 June 2004

Five minutes to five. Just woke up thinking of something Jeremy said yester-day about the total simplicity of his wedding, done with no ceremony at all, a sort of immediate essential, too important for any elaboration which would have seemed to be no more than flummery. That thought of authenticity came together with the notion about intense attention to the particular, anything from a ketchup bottle to a Bellini, which is the only way to eliminate the incongruities between objective depersonalised transcendent views of the state of things and the subjective self-absorbed view which they belittle, but which you need to keep close to hand. Non-egocentric attention to the particular. I recalled the footnote in which Nagel thanks a friend, I suppose a friend or a colleague, for getting him to feel this. A footnote being a fine suggestion of how he lived the discovery of this, rather unexpectedly perhaps. Coming quickly, without trappings. And then these two, the account of the nature of the wedding and the notion about attention to the particular, chimed with, simply, the view I had as I stood up and looked out of the window at the street in what I at once recognised as that early morning light that is experienced as the illumination of the world before anything in it has got going, begun to play its part. That cold light which has stopped me before, often, making me hold a breath or two, even before breakfast in hot summer weather. It takes away the comfort of things, the acceptability of them, so they stand stark as nothing much at all. You know you are passing through, leaving it behind almost at once. In this case there was the end wall of the house opposite, modern pale bricks with a scatter of cheap orange, cream and darker ones, unimpressive, the locust tree over there, which I now saw was mostly dead with only a couple of sprays leafing, also the gardens receding along the cul-de-sac, and a half hidden house at the far end of that row, with scaffolding and a notice on that saying 'Sky Hi', a commercial gesture, but far off, and thus small, just legible, stating but not pushing itself, in spite of its intentions. Authenticity. The stripped down. The fright of the matter-of-fact, but coupled with, this time, an undecorated urgency, a delight of knowing you really don't need much of a ceremony. This combination I had not felt so well before, and it stayed with me to give clarity to the morning.

Peter and Beryl, before they set off back to Cambridge, came with us to South Elmham, the Minster, on Sunday morning. The rain held off, though the sky was heavy. We parked on the concrete standing, as usual, and walked west and south to the Minster, and, once again, I have to remind myself about what is thought about it. That the building could be eleventh-century, because of the freestone slab found in the wall, a gravestone, but that the form of the architecture could be earlier, seventh- or eighth-century. The notice on the site had opted for the later date and attributed it to Herbert de Losinga. It had the narthex described as a tower. I re-read both Warner and Harrold when we get home and once more get the feeling of that odd area, the Saints.

Nothing much happened when we were there, but the nothing much included hares, big ones, two of them being chased across a field by a long-haired black dog, as we approached the turn south into the track coming in. They were not having to unwind themselves very vigorously, and kept plenty in reserve for sudden accelerations. Later, and again on the way out, in that long, narrow field that leads to the ruins, one, or possibly both hares were hanging around, coming into the open away from the hedges, loping a little, even giving occasional leaps. Just sufficiently so for it to feel odd. It would have been much more natural, more usual, if they had disappeared after being chased. They seemed to have been sent packing by the highly excited dog, then they were there again, unhidden, unexpectedly visible. Nobody would be surprised by rabbits emerging to go on feeding, but they would seem intent on business easily accounted for. The hares were as if checking something we didn't know about, something not as immediately evident as food to eat.

Hares play. They leap up. Leaping up is the essence of opening. 'Open' and 'up' are the same word. Intuition is a hare. It brings its transformations, making the rationally impossible happen, startling in its appearance. John Layard said so. These did seem large, ready to unleash themselves if that seemed to them the thing to do, touched up bravely with black and white, and truly remarkable for length of back leg. They are supposed to enjoy being hunted, even if there could scarcely be a more obvious piece of wishful thinking. These were flaunting themselves while pretending not to see us, as the four of us walked up the middle of the field, talking. The Iceni, who owned this territory, used them as portents. Boudicca loosed one from her garments to watch how it would run and so foretell the outcome of the battle. And it has been taken to be unlucky to meet one. The bad luck needs the next meal to cancel it. Well, it was sad to see the Rileys leave at the end of that little holiday. But I need more. I need some spirits to glimpse, some oddities, some significations that there is more here than matter of fact, and they do strike me as peculiar, there between the ancient hornbeams, near the Roman ditched enclosure and the possibly Saxon Minster, where, on a long-ago visit, I remember there was a dead crow in the atrium and, more years ago still, a huge brown cricket on the remains of the chancel. And so today, 13th, Tuesday, because I have been reading about it, Barbara and I extend a shopping-trip into Halesworth by driving on to Rumburgh, past the Priory church, and turning right to park in Uncle's Lane, to walk where it is a track running north. Uncle's Lane. Uncle. Uncouth. The strange lane that leads on to Flixton and the higher ground, where there are, close together, Neolithic post holes and Bronze Age tumuli, or the remains of them, a lane that, if projected south, comes down to end at the Buck's Head Inn.

We follow it for a field or two, until it slims into a single-file track through corn, then meets a cross path where there is a coppice of maples and oaks. Then we turn back. It was the end of this track, where it meets the road, where, five years ago, we walked, briefly, on the day when we were deciding if we ought to make an offer for a house in Rumburgh or come to Bramfield. At that time we knew nothing of its being a prehistoric track, nothing of Uncle. Today there is what you would expect, hardcore spread in the wheel ruts where the track is wide, with grass up its spine and a shallow ditch on the west with a strip of growth between it and the track. Hardheads, meadow thistle, which smells of honey if you pinch its flowers, clumps of bedstraw, swathes of pink lesser bindweed, and half a dozen small tortoiseshell butterflies landing on the path in front of us, spreading open their yellow and orange and blue and black, then flitting up and landing again further ahead, until we come up with them and they repeat the process. A lively, but limited company. In the corn further on, the ears are ripening, making crackling sounds in the hot sun. Flat horizon, the top of St Michael's tower in trees, at first, then, at our furthest, St Peter's just rising into view. No hares.

There is a grim sort of pleasure in this landscape, so stripped down and simplified, and the power given by this stripping down is given to what is left, such as the flints in the soil, white or black or brown, split or knobbed, and the open flashes of the butterfly wings. There are often three or four skylarks which rise and sing, sometimes two close together. At the top of their climb, they stiffen their wings, float level for a distance, then turn down and plummet. They were doing it, were they, 4,500 years ago, when people walked this track, heading for the higher ground on the northern skyline, with their illusions that matter-of-fact was not all there was to it? Uncuo. Strange, or unfriendly. Weird. Matter spread out almost flat. Wings that flicker at your feet. The popping sound of swollen seed cases. All this seems to be holding back, stopped in its tracks, caught hard and dry within itself. No ecstasy, just the slightly astonishing ferocity in the lark's dive down at the earth, a somewhat desperate curving attack. Or the sense that the spread of quick colour in the butterfly wings is a blink, as you meet, momentarily, face to face. Life itself was weird, the Saxons felt. Is this a possibility? Today I like very much this all that there is. I would come back for it.

14 November 2004

Tim comes on his own today, leaving Sam to play Sunday football. He set off from Cambridge at 8 am and arrived here at 9.30 as we were about to have breakfast, so he seemed to be here all day, going again at 8.30 in the evening when the puddles were still not frozen. The whole time was windless and silent, even at Covehithe and Dunwich Heath. At the former so much cliff has fallen that the beach is mostly sand. Long waves hold onto themselves until the final break, then come down heavily, recoiling round the black stumps of old trees rooted in the beach. The mergansers are on the Broad, on the far side, and distinguished by lowness in the water, some chestnut round the head, a vermilion flash, sometimes, from the wet beak. Little auk, we are told, are arriving off the sea. Winter is coming, and the open ocean north of Iceland has a weighty presence to bear down on us. It feels as if these long waves come from that, rolling with the momentum of tipping south, having to ripple all the way until they get to the end. Little auk nest in fissures in cliffs that are snow-bound even after the eggs have hatched. They shelter in loose talus and are often iced in before they can move south. Iceland, says the old book. No longer, says the new one. Siberian Arctic, Greenland, Alaska. Follows cold currents and likes to be amongst broken floes.

We walk south of the Covehithe road, with Southwold on the horizon, its pier clear of the sea and in silhouette. The field runs to the cliff and over it a flock of larks is swirling. A piece of dead, black and white detritus is floating a few yards out from the surf, but it is… alive. Its hunched head turns, altering the white shape of its chin and lower face. It is squat and huddled, exactly as in the illustrations. There are no others. It peers around as if in pain. Then it flies, with rapid energy and sharp wings, setting off to the north.

We eat at the White Horse in Westleton, as we used to thirty years ago There is the same row of jugs round the ceiling, the same propeller in the centre, in case of hot days. Different customers, but arranged in familiar ways, with the knot of men, regulars, at the left end of the bar, one woman amongst them, and other women eating at the table against the north window. Sunday roast, either pork or beef.

Then, eventually, to Dunwich Heath, to be on the car park above the cliffs in time to see the starlings again. They do it spectacularly, as the sun drops behind the woods. Five thousand, certainly, coming in parties to join the huge, speckled amoeba that bulges and pirouettes, tugs itself almost in two, then decides not to snap but to swing round from its centre and string out in one direction only, stretching thinner, then soaked up to something smaller and blacker, snatching up its skirts, rearing up, swooping and shooting open to fill the sky, all noiseless, then coagulating, bursting, rattling into the reeds and, now, chattering there, so loudly that you can't hear the sea. Last time there was a solitary, silver hen-harrier which left the trees, flew into the flock where it was thickest, and came right through it without making a contact.

14 January 2005

One could ask oneself why one was frightened. This would risk finding something which makes it more frightening once found. What is there here to discover? Whatever it is will surely come first as an image, a memory. It will come with an uneasiness difficult to pin down rather than an extended mood. The uneasiness will be the more disturbing because it will insist that it is there to be clarified if you go into it further.

Already I have an image. A duck is turning on water, holding its head high and slightly tilted, looking about. It is a drake scaup, and I saw it on Benacre Broad the day before yesterday. Its head was dark, but definitely cobalt turquoise, precisely that, as a gloss on the dark feathers. The green of a mallard but not so green, more hidden. And wet, because the bird had just surfaced from a dive. It is January, and cold. The water must be numbingly cold. The bird rows itself around, curving across the choppy wavelets. I doubt if it matters that it is a scaup, beyond the fact that I would not have been looking at it so carefully had it been a mallard. Or, perhaps, what I am thinking now gives importance to the precise image if it, though, before I thought it, each detail did not matter so much.

The duck was not in any way close to me. I was a watcher. No matter what the physical distance was between myself and the bird, no matter that I was seeing it through binoculars so that what was there was very clear, the distance between us was absolute and the bird was unreachable. Once noticed, this distance was not only a feature of the scaup on the water, it instantly became the way the water's urgency conveyed itself, made its way past, in detail, sky blue dropped on it, silver flash and flink off it, and cold, of course, but not at all close. In fact unreachable. Also the cold, stiff, scratchable wood of the planks of the hide. You could work on them, pry off splinters or run your thumb on the smooth edge of the shutter, twist the metal butterfly nut that held the shutter open, a rather rusty nut, which wobbled on its screw, but none of this would bring anything closer. No closer than the cobalt turquoise shine, way out there on the scaup's head, turning about, sleeked with wet. Someone had collected rubbish from the beach, scraps of fishing net, polystyrene packing, in a plastic sack, and had left it just inside the door of the hide, where it rustled and jerked in the wind. Sudden, jumpy, squeaky sounds, which you could not hope to hold close.

Maybe, when something feels close in the way I am looking for, one feels that some heed has been taken of it, to hold it and keep it. Ostensibly this was true of the items in the bag of rubbish, but not in the important way. They were only left as collected. When the requisite heed is not being taken things are loose, however rigidly they keep still, however they flap in the wind. There is no guarantee that they are firm. Hard, probably. Cold, yes. Wet after a dive. All of it in quite bright January winter light, with nothing to depress you in that, other than the clarity of it, which showed so much, but did not cheer. However, they are not given the close guarantee. They hold a position only because there seems no such thing as being 'in position'. They take place though there seems nothing that can be 'in place', properly. I suppose this is it. Things had just come, and, having done that, there was no closer to come.

Close. Clause. Shut into clauses. In sentences. Of course one can interfere with the lack of closeness by writing about it. You close in on the head of the scaup like that. But it loses the quality it had before it seemed possible to write about it, which was that it was not close, that it was not coming closer, that it was, all the time you were aware of it, coming away. Being nearer, physically, often makes things further away. Nothing is more distant than the sunlit hairs on the back of my hand, which glimmer like the gloss on the scaup's head. And perhaps an experience 'comes off' only before it is possible to write about it, when 'comes off' carries a twofold suggestion, first the shock of the happening, the chance of its coming about, of events coming off that way, turning out to be unexpectedly 'in place', secondly the sense of something going, slipping away, getting loose, falling off. The arrival and the loss feel bound to happen together.

Today Barbara catches a train for London, for Birmingham, for Shenstone, for her moderators' meetings. A woman on the platform at Darsham Halt wears suede boots, and their pelt-like texture is out on the concrete, not close. A transparent plastic sack is hanging from a metal collar fixed to the brick wall of the platform shelter. Like the sack in the hide. It contains a rolled magazine, and another plastic bag, this one opaque yellow. Though it is crushed now, this is a larger bag than the one containing it. The ensemble swings in the wind and knocks against the wall, urgently and unpredictably. It is stiff enough to knock rather than rustle. It is not 'absurd', though I suddenly realise that might be what I am about to conclude. There is no doubt about its function, or the usefulness of its function, and today I don't feel as if such usefulness is absurd. But its usefulness is not very heedful, so it is now feeling left, far off, very easily explicable, but discounted. Barbara gets on the train, into carriage B, to find her numbered seat. The window glass is dark and reflective so only the merest shadow of her passing down the coach is visible, but, as the train hoots and pulls away, there am I, sunlit and vividly detailed, facing myself, being left. For a second there is something closer, face on, as

I recognise myself in the process of coming off, peeling away into more of the gloss on the hairs and the feathers. I can write about leaving the station, the more easily because it can be a narrative, as I pass through the white gate in the palings, brush dry mud off the small piece of carpet I keep under my feet in the car, take hold of the steering wheel. Writing will give that fake sort of closeness, which I know won't be enough. Probably if these things were absurd, which none of them are, they would be harder to write about and they might 'come off' better.

I'll try a little further with this, since it comes back to me when I think of Benacre two days ago. Robert was with me and we had started the day at Sotterley, hoping for hawfinches, but there was only a glimpse of a nuthatch, short tailed, in mid air between trees, and we walked out across the fields, through the dozen or so huge oaks, decrepit, dramatic, white in the sunlight, eventually to the church, into which we stepped, in case anything had happened in there since we came before. January. It was bleak in there with no heat at all, but also no wind, no draught. What 'came off' this time were the regimental banners suspended at the back of the nave. Like so many such banners, they had gone thin. The flesh had dropped off them. The fibre, the elaboration, the surface of coloured stuff, had dusted away, without, one imagined, their having moved at all while it happened. Not a ripple. Hung out there until large pieces of them had become spectral chiffon, tea-coloured gauze, though in other places they were still plumper, scarlet and gold and blue, though dirty. They were of a Scottish regiment, presented to an officer from hereabouts. Full, then, of heedfulness. Full of as much meaning as possible. 'The Peninsula' it said amongst the folds. And 'Waterloo'. Were they the actual flags carried through the breeze at Waterloo? I thought not, but Robert was of the opinion they were. Suppose, then, that they were. Suppose I take it that what he said was valid, as his quiet voice suggested it ought to be. At this point I need, for some reason, to remember that there had also been a barn owl, a white one, dirtied with grey, flying up in the wood by the field as we neared the church. Close, but, of course, far off, the further because of its suddenness. Side view. Flat face. Tail view. Gone. Bleached white. As old as the flags. Owls are further away than most birds, however close you get, and I mean, chiefly, barn owls. It is because so much heedful effort has gone into getting close to them, as into the flags. Barn owls carry plenty of significance of the sort most birds escape from altogether. A barn owl in this winter wood.

Waterloo banners in the nave. The heavy door clunks. In the cold, still heart, it all 'comes off' and mostly so because it emphatically did, in the first way, and, in the second way, it was never intended to, it was intended that it definitely should not come loose. Waterloo came off. An owl, which you disturbed when you had no expectation of such a bird, came loose, loose, loose. Quite early on Wednesday morning, a normal weekday, with plenty of time for us to go on to Covehithe, Benacre, and the chef's roast at the Five Bells.

13 February 2005

For two seconds I register a bird's head which is raw sienna, with, on its shoulders below that, burnt umber. And a huge, pale beak. One hawfinch, sorting through the dead leaves, accompanied by a dozen greenfinch, all hunched and scuffling where the bank rises between the roots of a hornbeam. The sunlight has slanted in. Then some alarm and they volley off, past the trunk and high into the open. A year and two days ago was the last time I saw hawfinch. That, also, was on the edge of this stand of trees. This ramification, fanning to the thin hornbeam twigs, black twigs in front of hurried rain cloud today, and some quickly remodelled exposures of blue sky. Soon we are overcast and pills of hailstones are jumping across the grass. Three times this week, here at Sotterley, there has been the barn owl out there, in the morning, in the afternoon, over the rotten, soaked fields.

Robert Bresson said that the actor, learning his part, presupposes a self which he knows in advance, who is really a self who does not exist. I must mind my business more and take more care to exist. Notice more and stop scripting it. No more writing for gawps. No more 'huge beak' or 'volley off' or even 'jumping hail'. Too much bird watching and too much weather. 'Classified as creatures of chaos', birds were, by the Egyptians, and there needs to be brisk picking off. I need Seneb's wand, her throwstick.

Target. Coccothraustes coccothraustes. Here's a chance. Hit it. 'Continues to be very rare'. So hit it. 'Reported from just seven locations this year'. Hit it. Sienna and umber; raw and burnt. Colour it. The big, pale bill 'which exercises forces in excess of 50 kgm'. Feel the pinch poking about in the loose leaves. The face is tilted, glaring down, intently, amongst the leaves, with the rest of the bird hidden behind humped ground. Its acid green companions are equally busy. In the instant they all leap upwards, to the left, and I am refocused on some black dots in the tops of distant oaks. No lines to learn. The pellets of hail are looking very lively over the trodden grass. 'Just there', Heller said in 1969, 'pounding the table / spilling the drink / I bought for you'. There is still more to be made of those sixties and the readiness to pound and spill. Don't cuddle the drinks. 'Don't write nature poetry', shouts the horny blue bill.

17 April 2005

There is a small Veronese exhibition in the Correr. He is not a painter to always enthral me, but always there has been the great Hermes, Herse and Aglauros in the Fitzwilliam, exceptional, blue and silver, wonderful to me for forty years. At first this exhibition seems rather desperate, limited, with its climax fetched in from nearby, the freshly cleaned Europa, which is, of course, luscious. That will be in the last room, the inner room, well spotlit. But, when we get in there, there is first, opposite this, smaller, 109 by 90.2 cm., from Vienna, the Lucrezia. Yes. 1583. Five years before he died. A late work into which he was allowing explicit emotion. I have seen illustrations of this. Here it is.

Face down-tilted and eyes lowered. Her lips are notably unmoved as the sword goes in. She hides the cold hurt. The lack of overt expression is not, at any rate, any longer just his style, the vestige of mannerism. It registers tragedy. True, but however true, the colours do still decide that she belongs to Veronese. The crackly old-gold cloth through which she pushes the blade. Then the main dress, thick cloth, viridian, Hooker's green, dark. Underneath this is lined pink, but you see only a slender thread of that at the hem, where it is caught up over the furniture, over the frame of the bed on which she sits. And there is a scarf-width of another cloth draped on this, next to the green, just a twist of it at the right edge of the picture. It is thinly striped silver and what looks like light blue. Glittering silver. A blue which, when you look at it, has a core of cobalt green, and there is a double, thick stripe, down near its fringe, of olive, shadowed to umber. Veronese choosing colours, colours so evidently chosen that they certainly are mannerist. You acknowledge his demonstration. Place this scarf. You see him do it.

Then there is the tapestry curtain bellying down, top right. It is curled through by embroidered stems and pods and flowers, but dimmed. Sap green. Terre vert. Very grey turquoise. Light Hooker's green. The rims of the petals and buds and leaves are softly sparkling pink and rose thread, taking up the pink from the thread of the robe's lining below. Shadowed. So. Old-gold, deep blue-greens, one spurt of sky blue and silver. Also the glimpses of the edges of her creamy white blouse, rucked. Her golden hair. Gold metal—her bracelets and the hilt of the sword. And, of course, pearls, on her hair, and alight in the shadow of her chin. One big ruby on her hair, the only intense red, but referred to again by the blood seep on the blade, down centre, between her hands. Just beginning to gleam down there. A thin, black bootlace coming loose from a plait of her hair. The wood of the bed seen in the gap in the cloth, looking mauve in the gallery light, but actually sepia and neutral tint. It is flushed with reflected colour. And flesh. Bare shoulders, forearms. The right side of the canvas is filled, all cloth. The left is empty blackness and her face and shoulder and white sleeve are against that. And, fixing the picture, the blue and silver scarf. She kills herself in his colours. A full mix of very subdued, rich sadness, and the scarf.

The obvious complement to green, red, is hived into the ruby, faded into the flush on the curtain, slipped in on the pink thread. The challenge, instead, is more dissonant, the rag of bright silver and blue. What does this do to the sadness? Provokes it. Gives it a twinge. Twists it to taste. A masterstroke. He chose Titian not Tintoretto when he arrived in Venice, avoiding the ascendant Venetian mannerism of active, muscular, diagonal, electric posturing. Then he showed what he could do with Titian. Rich. But with a shrewder thrill. Nothing in S. Sebastian, where we go afterwards because the whole church was decorated by him... nothing there to take away this time. Hooker's green. A flash of blue. Stabbing herself quietly.

17 and 20 April 2005

As we are in San Giovanni Crisostomo it begins to rain heavily. Again the altarpiece requires coins in a box to work the lights. For a moment I think the coins play music too, but Beryl points out that the music does not synchronise with the light.

This could be one of the greatest paintings in the world. I have believed Wollheim's assertion without ever being here before. I find such assertions important. They up the stakes. It is the last picture he deals with in his 1984 lectures, the Bellini, which is of great expressive simplicity but of a pictorial subtlety which nothing he has said so far has prepared for. He was pleased to end the lectures upon it. He spent hours with it. On this trip I am determined to spend considerable time here. He must have had hundreds of 50 cent pieces. I rubbish the thought and begin. I am here. To see, I suppose, what I have been told. To begin by doing that.

What does it mean, and why should it matter, that a picture should 'metaphorize' the body? Today I take a clue from earlier than Wollheim, thinking of Adrian Stokes, who talked about how, in paintings, foreground figures seem to be convex and backgrounds concave. He suggested that we seek part-object relationships as we enter and search about in the concavity, but stand back and are confronted by the convex foreground figure, accepting it as itself, not defending ourselves by splitting, accepting it as complex and self-sufficient. And, sometimes, the whole picture can step up to us like that, asserting itself. I presume that, then, the picture has 'metaphorized' the body, which we face as a totality in its own right, seeing the mother for herself. Something of that. It will get me a start.

At first I am only aware that there is no disappointment at all. The two foreground standing saints assimilate to the piers they stand against. They carry weight, as the piers carry the arch. The Christ on Christopher, the heavy clothes on Louis. They carry weight easily. The two piers, the saints as piers, the marble parapet between them and the huge detailed, horizontally stratified rock lying across above that, add to each other, enhance each other, and come up as a metaphor for, as a piece of, classical architecture, edge to edge, solid and full and levelled and facing you all together. Jerome, up there sitting above the rock, framed by the arch, against the evening sky, seems to move forward to be beneath the arch that is well in front of him. Having the arch framing him does that. He is in the open air beyond, but he feels to be moved forward closer to us. The whole picture closes up forwards, steps to meet you, as a strongly conceived classical façade, head on, which doesn't leak anywhere, but confronts and advances. Jerome's simple profile and silhouette do not suck at or swallow the rest of the picture and you can, most fantastically, and I can't want to say why, assume that all the scenery behind him in the mountains is spread inside his mind, and is proffered to us by his thought, fetched from there, where it is, in the distance, to be more a part of the whole thing, the whole picture as one equal thing, far and near and edge to edge, brought forward against this actual space in San Giovanni, up close to the benches in the small nave.

Nobody speaks. There is absolutely nothing to ignore, from the rock plants to the mountains. And nothing in this world that could be mocked. My grandfather, who taught me the names of the stars, and read with me in the encyclopaedia so that maybe the first word I knew was 'hippopotamus', would have taken this picture most seriously. Christ ducks and peers over Christopher's head, looking beyond us to our left, making little or no claim on us, beyond the fact that He does not want us to look at Him. He is cautious, a bit of truth that you notice along with the spleenwort on the rock. He needs care. St Louis looks beyond us to our right. Christopher looks up above us. We are included so centrally, faced up to, by not being picked on, by being passed on all sides.

Back again, a day or two later. For all the afternoon. That satisfaction. Hello to it, to having the time.

Jerome is outside in the huge evening space, where there is no wind disturbing the fig leaves or the pages of his book. The mountains are miles away, but, at their most distant, they dip above Christ, so the gamboge hue, the cadmium yellow of the bottom of the sky, comes close to Him, as does the light on the left hand pier's capital. From front and back light gathers there, without fuss, as He curls round behind the darkness of Christopher's hair. There is level rose cloud along the low horizon and a single corkscrew of thicker, darker grey and rose across higher up, across behind Jerome's shoulders and lit from underneath by the afterglow. The sky rises deeper into evening blue. You can feel Jerome in that slightly surprising condition of being outside when outside is as still as inside, but much more cool and capacious. And then the two standing saints, right and left, are on the threshold of the building, of this building, looking in, backs to the evening outside. Light falls from front right, much as if from the chapel window alongside the picture, here in San Giovanni, and throws their shadows aslant and back over a tiled floor, a narrow ledge of it, in front of the arch and the parapet. They are coming inside this building, yet welcomed by light from our side, whatever the logic of its source. Jerome brings the outside in to us, a still evening into a still building. The open opens in insideness.

The brightest fragment of white is the bottom corner of the far page of Jerome's book, where the page curves up from the spine. It is a fang of white, under his outstretched hand, as if he were reaching for a pearl as he went to turn his page. From his point of view, though not from ours, the whole double page he is reading must be as white as that, written on snow. Where does this brightness come from? Too hard to say. From some portion of the sky hidden by the arch? But why should there be a source of bright light up there? One far off tower in the foothills is white like the bit of the page, the distant tower and the near page, a pair of small bright studs fixing the journey in to the look across. I remember that his Agony in the Garden in London is a scene lit from the front, so that the walls of Jerusalem glow, though there is a sunset beyond them.

Some of the plants could be ivy-leaved toadflax. The most prominent have small white flowers like rock cinquefoil. There is definitely one spray of Asplenium. Spattered detail fledges in the clefts, all worthwhile and there to be noticed. When the artificial light flicks off, and you have no more coins, you can, now that it is afternoon, and there is no more rain, get used to the natural light and still see, without so much gloss, and this gives you more time. How did Bellini intend it to be lit? Some candles? But it is better that it should not flicker. So long as you stand left of centre to throw bouncing light from the chapel window away from the picture, it will all do. A priest can't believe we don't want the electrics. Beryl and Peter have turned up and joined me again. We sit in the pews.

The figures in the altarpiece are, I think, life size. Did I know they were so big? Next week, cutting the lawn in sunshine, I can still see them clearly without shutting my eyes. The painting moves towards me across the grass, its colours in the air, still enhancing each other, the rose and the brown and the green.

18 April 2005

The right hand gryphon on the tomb of Giacomo Surian in Santo Stefano is bigger than the left. Their expression, open beaks, tongues laid flat inside them, heads cocked aside, eyes rolled up, is not rage, but certainly they hiss a warning which keeps me expectant, feeling watched, checked on, close to fierce attentions. At lunchtime, however, we walk beside a canal where the water is milky green and unruffled. Someone has dropped a white, fully inflated balloon, and it skims along the surface, the nipple acting as a rudder, dragging in the surface film, a pivot, so that when the wind wavers the balloon swerves left or right. It moves along as fast as you can walk, keeping abreast of a party of people on the far bank. Then it steers in between a barge and the wall and sticks. There are hoses, yellow or blue, looped up alongside some sections of canal, carrying whatever, sewage even, as required by work being done. The blue hose is more intense blue than anything in a Veronese, or any other picture. You could not afford anything so blue in a picture. It soaks a hole in the scene, as if something had scratched across the visual field and this blue was the colour of the seepage swelled up through the scratch. Suddenly the white buildings move, are moving, and it is a liner on the Giudecca across the end of the street. Small spectators line the deck up there, looking down into the city.

An elderly Irish woman, thin haired, lost, is crouching on the steps at the end of a bridge, over her map, which, she says, is 'in tatters'. She asks another woman the way to the Accademia. The second woman sits by her to look at the map, but there is no need because there is a yellow and black sign to the Accademia immediately on the wall across the bridge. She is flustered, God blesses us, and stops as she moves off up the steps, behind the woman who helped her, to look down on her head and say 'I like your hair.' This has been bleached in streaks. 'Thank you.' How big, in the scheme of things, are such encounters? They seem sometimes to register on the same scale as does falling in love. At other corners old women crouch, heads down, holding out small pots for money, or a younger woman steps up to you, crying softly, then, immediately, moves off, still crying, to try someone else. Or a brown, tanned man in a black cloak sits playing a cello, watching you closely as you pass. Your guilt calls them witches, and hopes they forget you immediately.

The pigeons scuttle with coral legs, white stone rumps and emerald and purple gloss on their necks. They often fly hard and low, just missing your head. One has a thread of shit stuck trailing out of its arse. A female sparrow fizzes and hops on your café table, so you want to beat it away as if it were diseased. Gulls stand with perfect poise on the tops of posts. Wellheads are hot and glassy at the rim, cut and carved, the soak holes to take rainwater down into the sunken tanks punched through stone slabs at a distance around them. The chiselled plaques, chunky or delicate, set into the facades, between windows, over doorways, which are crosses, pateras, protoma, family crests, shields, and which show paired animals, eagles, pelicans, angels, an Annunciation, a Byzantine emperor, a monk with some pupils kneeling in front of him, a cat with a bird… they advertise, boast, drive off illnesses or demons, and brooch the vertical, as the wells do the horizontal. Their ambience is echoing, physically and mentally. They are ancient and splendidly well done, each of them, and it will be a pity if any one of them is forgotten, or neglected because of a shop window display of open boxes filled with a range of intensely bright powdered paints, or gloves, all fixed upright and giving you signals. The landing stages for the vaporetti rock, always, and the one nearest to us, at San Samuele, creaks as it rocks, even when nobody is on it, night and day. It creaks. The police were gathered here in the dark on Friday, waiting for something, probably not the creaking.

There is a pair of fat, triangular earrings in a jewellers along the street, semi-precious stones, or even glass, citrine, a pale lemon set in thick silver, which Barbara does not want. My ring, silver with its square carnelian, comes into action wherever there is preciousness or colour, so that I am glad of it. It is a utility. I hold it up and engage it with the other colours in the world. The Aquabox lavatory cistern in the flat overflows as it did last year. It is worth having for its name, with a 'q' and an 'x' in it, and for the notion of boxing up water, the ridiculous confidence that you might hold liquid in a plastic box, or in a canal. And also the leaping and punching and ducking of pugilism in the face of a mechanism that does not do what you require of it without repeatedly asserting its right to fail. But mostly the bathroom routine here has a marked satisfaction. To clean your razor by running it under hot water, holding it low, so the water falls hard on it and searches the cracks out, then washing the can of gel so that the deposit round its nozzle and inside its cap is cleaned out, and it is wet and hot and shining, to be dried and placed again, a survivor, on the ledge of the bath. Notable business, here, because it is in Venice, as the sun gets high enough to top the roof, come into the window, and the bells bong.

8 August 2005

The watercolours in the Cotman Gallery in the Castle Museum at Norwich are, of course, changed regularly. The present selection contains some of the very best. Cotman's own Marl Pit, for instance, Leman's Snowdon from Capel Curig, Bright's barn, done in Kent in 1847, and his chalk drawing of a cataract. 1847 was a year of brilliance I think, mostly because of John Middleton, who was in Kent, with Bright, and also in Norfolk, as witness his Water Gate at Alby, and the stream vanishing into a brick arch in a wood at Blofield, that year. Here today are several Middletons. There is a later, more worked up, more thickly and vividly coloured one, of Lynmouth, river with rocks, of 1850, regarded, say the notes, as being a little late for his best, but still shining. However, this morning and this afternoon, because I manage to take two sessions of an hour each, one before, one after lunch, there is this Study of Rocks and Trees, which I have not seen before. It must be about 1847, and it is a study, as it claims, but is as big as the Water Gate and the others.

Only the centre is brought to a finish. The left side is ghosted in, a rising track, the right an equally hinted slope falling away with sky open behind it. The foreground is out of focus rocks and clitter, done with the slightest washes and touches. The centre is thus presented as altogether important, with the feeling of air around your head as you look at it, space where you are not looking. It is a few large rocks with a tree bursting forward from a crevice between them. The tree appears as a lump composed of three globular gnarls clumped together to make one sphere, with two trunks springing and diverging from this, and also four lesser shoots, branch sized, sprouting from it. It carries another shoot that has been chopped, and a protruding knot with a hole in it. The knobbed sphere is composed of the bulges grown tightly together, with squeezed cracks between them, complex curved and graduated surfaces with pockets and wedges and small shelvings on them and in them, some of them caught green where lichen is being found out by the sun, which comes in from your right. The shadows of the stems are thrown over this complexity in perfectly unpredictable and obviously uninventable ways. This is the central event, with the branches kinking and twisting up from it, their exact directions and slopings never to be taken for granted, never rhythmically curved. Shadows jink over the individuality of the irregularities. The whole is done without any mess, everywhere with flair. It is not flicked on, but placed down quickly and steadily, with no fiddling or afterthoughts, edges precise, paint very thin.

Today no trees by anyone else in the gallery come near to this in giving me the poignant conviction that this is how it was, that nobody would invent it like this, that he found it. All other trees seem dirtier, dottier, splashier, wristy or mannered, more sentimental, picturesque, staged, mass produced, gesturing, compared to this. A tour of the corridor confirms me here. There are lovely things, Cotman's compositions in clear blocks of colour and so on, but nobody else has done the looking that was involved like this. A study. Indeed. If I look at Bright's Waterfall next to it, and then at Middleton's Lynmouth rocks and beach, I can see, or so I imagine, the same difference. The stones in Middleton have what you might call an awkwardness in the way they abut each other, pile a little against each other, lie askew next to each other, which awkwardness he tackles as it is, it forces him to do it as it is. Of course it does not make the painting look at all awkward, he does it so deftly, and takes his delight in it, but I see that he did not choose that the stones should lie like that to begin with, whereas Bright and the others, once they had got started, put them mostly as they felt the picture wanted them, chose the surfaces the picture could do with, the gaps that suited its requirements, the scatter that ran nicely for it, did they not? In Renaissance art, even Bellini does not look like this. His closest detail is trimmed and posed and displayed for you, by comparison. Middleton's tree is evidence of the value of consciousness bared to this degree. That is what it studies. I feel a sort of rage for it, on its behalf. I feel that it makes fools of those who pass down the corridor with only a glance, as it does of those who stroll down the lanes without being brought to a stop. Seeing it like this must matter. It must matter even if you move on, which I don't, deciding that you can't afford to get stuck in so much noticing, spending so much attention on getting to see it, and even to remember it. It shakes me. 'Know this', it says. 'Know it, and that makes at least two of us who do.'

Ruskin was born in 1819. The Pre-Raphaelites founded themselves in 1848. Holman Hunt did the Hireling Shepherd in 1851, Millais the Winchelsea background of The Blind Girl in 1854. These are assembled, set up, the Middleton tells me, this afternoon. They make a business of it. Where else could I go for what is here? It will be amongst the less noticed, the cooler, the slighter reputations, people who don't seem to be trying so hard for the impact. There is certainly George Boyce, At Binsey with those guinea fowl in the grass and the apple boughs breaking across the willows, the two sorts of leaves moving through each other, amazing me, a little later, in 1862. We went to Bedford for that, years ago, and to the Tate, to the Pre-Raphaelite landscape exhibition, last year. Leaves and grass do these things and they are not obvious. They need the long, unrehearsed look. And that place, Binsey, takes you to Hopkins, with his poplars and their haecceitas. Hopkins looked at Boyce 'at the Water-colours', as he says in his journal, July 2, 1866. 'Was at the Water-colours. ... Boyce's things as good as usual.' At Binsey. There is what matters. Boyce a little later, and, earlier, Middleton, both of them with their water colour skills, moving in without the evident stress and strain and piling up, without all the worry, letting the paper through, so they seem to get to it, smoothly and cleanly. This afternoon. Any Middleton at all that I can look at for an hour or two in the Cotman Gallery, but mostly this one, this Study of Rocks and Trees.

21 September 2005

We spent hours in the Egyptian rooms. A bronze Horus with his head emptied of its eyes and cheeks, its jewels and glass, and now like the hollow metal skull of a hawk. But he stands tall and steps forward, extending both arms in front of him, and his hands, his long fingers, his elegant, tricky fingers, stretching, the hands close together, one a little in advance of the other, the one behind close up to the palm of the forward one, but not touching it, a shaft of space between them, both hands with fingers extended, as if directing forwards a smooth, straight, invisible shaft, a spear of force, the shaft of which is let slide through the space between the two sets of fingers, between the palms, as it shoots ahead of him, levelled at something way off, a target way off in front, as he might have let go a pigeon to fly straight out at some distant point, but still feels the move of the pigeon's leap forward where it was, between his hands, stroking through his fingers, which are still stretched along it, along that spear of air where the bird went. He is sending an invisible stream of water towards the face of Pharaoh. Magical comfort. A long, smooth drink sent out through the air. Water as air. To open the mouth. 'Hail, thou god Tem, grant me the sweet breath which lives in your nostrils. I live. I am delivered. I come out like the lily of mother-of-emerald of the god Hetep, the lily of green felspar which blossoms at sunrise in the dawn wind.'

What of the draughts pushed through the tunnels of the metro across the platforms ahead of the trains? Or sucked behind them? Half warmed winds. What of the piping hot motorbike exhausts between the walls of the Rue des Dames? Or the exhalations pumped out of the nozzles shaking under the vans running their engines there, waiting to move forward a few feet more, close outside the hotel windows, thundering while you eat breakfast? What of the old breath, stirred by the fan which turns this way then that, in the corner of the bar of the Eldorado, flushing the film posters and the amateur paintings of nudes. No hope of a chirpy draught to perk the nipples of the scratched, grey plaster copy of the torso by Maillol set up in the corner. But the brown hands of the waiter cuddle and crush the bright white cloth which they use to wipe the table top, and tap the cups into position, and correct the lie of the blackberry coloured paper napkins in front of you. They position the glasses of orange juice. And what is the number of your room? And are you Australians? Air to the nostrils of Pharaoh, and water to his mouth. Let there be magical precision.

And this, although you get into the wrong lift and end up alone on a dark, empty platform deep in the Gare du Nord. Though luggage sticks in turnstiles. Though your seats have been taken. Though the girl at the desk is desolate, there being no taxis in Paris in this morning's rush hour. Though the last face you saw in the gallery was by Ludovico Carracci, that of St Hyacinth, no face like it in the history of art before, the extreme degree of immediate, violent life, concentrated in his head and hands in a 'surreal straining towards ecstasy', beyond the self, and frozen rigid in this state. 'Utterly unforgettable'. Glare and tendon and wrenching knuckles. Forget and forget.

Forget because. Because you will not suffer diminution. You will be offered the croissant, sweet mother of sustenance, by the bronze hand that obeys the number of your room. Which obtains, in the noisy place.

24 October 2005

Cellardyke, John Street, five thirty and it will be dark soon. There has been soaking, steady rain all day, total overcast until an hour ago, when some long, low clouds offered themselves in the south-east, but were quickly reassimilated in the featureless grey. This is a narrow street between sandstone terrace houses, some rendered, some textured with rusticated blocks, a few painted rather surprising colours. One is dark cobalt blue all over, another lemon yellow. Or were those in James Street? But most are just the ochre, or brown, or buff, or almost orange sandstone, squared tight and fitted. Windows are rimmed with stone or painted strips. The yellow one wears red lipstick. Several houses are empty, though. You pass close and see into their front rooms. Dry boards and plaster. Out here is the snapping, salted air, blowing hard against the constraint of the available space. Wet tarmac, and shoes judging the puddles. You squeeze round cars that have been pulled onto the pavement to leave some room for other vehicles to pass. Or you step round stone steps laid along the front wall to reach a raised front door. And here is what makes this seem as full of implication as a Mass in B Minor. If you look down one of the passageways through the south side terrace, there will be, filling the whole frame of the sandstone entry, motion, slow motion, black and white in heavy, heavy motion, only yards away and coming at you over low black rocks. The Firth of Forth, blown this way and smashing at its leading edge. Behind the foam you can see the Bass Rock miles off over there, can you? Down through the passageways, it could be, or certainly from the back gardens. The kelp is mashed and threshed and stinking immediately over the garden wall. It is the edge, storming, with this side-street, your late Monday afternoon, right here, under its hammer.

On the north side there are sometimes bays between terraces, small ones packed usually with parked cars, but, once, with a cherry tree, standing over most of its yellow leaves, and, further on, a plot of turned earth with rose bushes, the flowers in pink, soaked lumps. These bays have high, concrete backs, because the land rises steeply away from the sea. Russian vine flowers along the top of the concrete here.

And a minute, passionate bird is dashing at the house fronts, jumping at the walls. Flickering gold. Then there is a second one, following. They are shrieking thin shrieks at each other. Here, at a corner where the wind has

137

some occasion to stand still for a moment, you can hear them. Clear shrieks like a wet finger on glass. So the book will say. It is so. If you stand still, so the book will warn you, they might even land on you and, so hungry they are, they might search over the fabric of your coat on the chance of there being something to eat in its threads. Goldcrests come over from Scandinavia, come over the North Sea. These two jump and swirl over the plot of turned earth at your feet, then skirmish away down the terrace, still not spent, escaping the pile and the drive and the hammer, away down John Street, towards James Street, where it will very soon, you hope, be raining a little more gently, as the forecast promises, in the dark.

Somewhere along there, it would be good to supply them with a forest of pines.

1 November 2005

Grey-blue, squared stacks of slate make the piers of the small, flat bridge. Their sides, in shadow, are near to black. The side of the central one is the darkest feature in the picture. In front of it, half way to the picture plane, a row of large stones, or small rocks, lies across the current of the shallow stream, and they are almost as dark, and not quite blue at all. There are five main stones in this row, and the detail on the largest of them, a groove, a tiny step which corners forwards and back across its head, is the most tightly focussed detail in the picture, given with the most precise, thin stroke of exact shadow. A detail, but, once noticed, it is a delight to stake your attention on its precision, to feel the move of the tip of the brush that made it. Nowhere else in the picture is whiter than the flecks of spray off these stones and the little carpets of foam coming away from them. When the electric light in the gallery strikes across the picture's surface you can see this white is laid on impasto, a little proud.

To either side of the stream the boulders and low banks rise, not at all steeply, rendered quickly, deftly, softly, fading into the paper as they widen out. Their colours shift into those of dry concrete, buffs, shading to Davy's grey, with the touch of olive in it. Snowdon, three peaks, is far back on the horizon behind the bridge, palest grey-blue, pearl, faint, and this colour is also on the glassier reaches of the stream below, reflected there together with the white of the sky. Foreground and background have the same colours in them. The sky is without a mark. It could be bare paper. One feels that if all the colour in the scene pooled together and flooded up over the sky, the sky would scarcely dirty much, and the whole sheet would return to being a clean rectangle, just solid enough to stand up to you. A rectangle of pale light, full face. Empty, ordinary day. So narrow a range of modest colours seems to want to resolve itself again into the simplest compromise.

After more looking, it occurs to me that the largest freestanding rock in the stream bed, the one in front of the bridge's central pier, an oblong block set at a sideways tilt towards the space under the bridge's right hand span and already partly obscuring it, would, if allowed to follow its inclination, and if it were squashed, only slightly patted down, fit into and fill that space. At once the notion gathers momentum. It looks, too, as if the lesser bits and boulders in front of the central span, collected and piled, would probably fit into that space also. A proposition suggests itself. All the solid chunks in the picture would build into a smooth, complete wall, and, that done, become the whole smooth face of the sheet of paper, held firmly in its broad white mask, here in the gallery. Just as the colours would like to get together, so the shapes, the facets of rocks and slabs and blocks of stone all about in the scene, seem to relate to each other, to belong together. Or they seem as if they would do so, were some of them to be spun round somewhat, angled more this way or that, twitched judiciously. They are sufficiently alike to approximate to each other. So many rocks are somehow squared, obviously, that you are bound to see them in sequences. The pale, stretched wedge that is furthest from you, on the shoulder between two of the mountain peaks, has to do with the shape of the side of a slab, caught by the light, at the side of the stream near the row of black stones in the foreground. These two patches have the same tone, lie on the same background colour, and are sufficiently alike to speak at the same time. Once you have said to yourself that these things are so, they are inescapably so.

All this is, of course, only a notion. In a way it is important that it is not essentially true at all, and that this remains, most authentically, the view at Capel Curig just as Leman saw it in 1852. Geology made the rocks and any relationships they might have, tumbled and fractured as they were. He saw them from where he was. But the fantasy of a further cohesion of what is here on the paper has suggested itself against this resistance. It is what you want, and you want the resistance too, and so did he, watching his picture. The record, and the fantasy of a further cohesion.

Time for an early lunch. Across to the room that is now a café, to eat beef stew with a dumpling, framed in a bowl, and drink a glass fitted full with freshly squeezed orange juice. Then, rather vaguely, I walk round the British Museum's travelling exhibition of Buried Treasure and see again the Mildenhall Great Dish, heavy, silver, and silvered with reflections, beaded, round, with Hercules and Pan and Bacchus and the glaring face of Oceanus in the centre. Here are piles of everyday metal objects, and holy things, bits of toys and green bronze axes, poured coins, a half-crushed gold cup, a shield that was doubled up but has been unfolded, patted back into shape, the skeleton of a man who came from abroad to die with Stonehenge as his immediate background. And, after the hoards and the stew, back to the picture, until I have completed exactly the right time so that I have enough left for me to wind my way down from the castle, out through the city, to the car park and meet Barbara. Bits and bowls, food and cups, crushing and uncrushing. Gods in dishes. Click the button and the car doors will open. Now what about the Mountain Landscape with Snowdon in the Background, by Robert Leman, 1852, one of the 'finest water colours in the school', which I have often seen but of which, today, I took some more heed?

Lightning Source UK Ltd.
Milton Keynes UK
UKHW011135300621
386402UK00001B/242